Making It on Your First Job

Making It on Your First Job

When You're Young, Ambitious, and Inexperienced

Revised Edition

Peggy Schmidt

Peterson's Guides
Princeton, New Jersey

Library of Congress Cataloging-in-Publication Data

Schmidt, Peggy J.
    Making it on your first job : when you're young, ambitious, and inexperienced / Peggy J. Schmidt. — Rev. ed.
        p.   cm.
    Includes bibliographical references.
    ISBN 1-56079-051-2
    1. Vocational guidance. I. Title.
HF5381.S355   1991
650.14 — dc20   91-9125

Composition and design by Peterson's Guides

Cover design by Jacqueline Steiner Adam

Printed in the United States of America

10 9 8 7 6 5 4 3 2

To my family —

Eddie, Phyllis, Gary, Thomas, Robert,
and Sherie

Contents

Acknowledgments

It is an author's dream to have a book she believes in live a second life, and for that I am indebted to Jim Gish, editorial director of Peterson's. Many thanks, too, to Charles Granade and Owen O'Donnell, whose editing of this revised edition was impeccable.

I would also like to restate my thanks to Carol E. Rinzler, whose support and editing of the first edition of the book helped make it the success that it was. The advice and suggestions given by my husband, Joe Tabacco, were likewise invaluable.

In addition to those people mentioned by name in the book, many thanks also go to the following people, particularly for their help in updating the information in this edition:

The American Management Associations
Nancy Carson, Program Manager at the Office of Technology
    Assessment
The College Placement Council
Crystal-Barkley Corporation
Dobisky Associates
John D. Erdlen, Executive Director, Northeast Human Resources
    Association
Gerry Everding, Washington University
Leonard Klein, Associate Director of Career Entry for the
    U.S. Government Office of Personnel Management
National Commission on Cooperative Education
National Institute for Work and Learning

Introduction: Why Should You Read This Book?

College graduates who will be looking for their first "real" job in the 1990s will find that there is both good news and bad news out there. First, the bad: There are still more job hunters with a degree than there are jobs requiring one. The competition to get a job that requires a college education is not as keen as it was in the baby boom era of the seventies and eighties. Still, hundreds of thousands of jobs that were once filled by high school graduates are now being awarded to college graduates, who employers feel have a good work ethic and desirable attributes like reliability, punctuality, and the ability to learn on the job.

Now, the good news: The tuition you paid and the hard work you did in college are worth the investment. Why? Because the more education you have, the more money you can earn. In the last decade, the earnings of college-educated males between the ages of 24 and 34 increased by 10 percent; those of women increased 15 percent. The earnings gap between white collar professionals (who hold the kind of job you will no doubt get or move into) and skilled tradespeople is at its biggest ever: 37 percent. Even greater is the earnings gap between professional and clerical workers: 86 percent.

Beyond the salary differential is another important fact: You are more likely to find work that challenges you and that you feel is interesting. More than eight in ten college graduates who work in professional or technical jobs are optimistic about their ability to achieve their career goals, compared with seven in ten other American workers. And they say the two most important factors about their current job is the amount of independence they have and the gratification of the work itself.

Depending on the kind of work you choose and where you look for a job, you may experience difficulty landing a first job — or the kind of first job that you had hoped for — because of a regional or industry-related business turndown. But no matter how daunting the odds may seem to get the first job of your dreams, keep in mind that *there are always good jobs to be had* if you know how to go about getting them. That means knowing what kind of job you want and deploying your entire arsenal of job-hunting resources. This book will help you choose a career and identify and learn to use employment skills.

Persistence will get you the job you want. Prospective employers will ignore you, put you off, even tell you "No" — all the more reason not to be deterred. That's not to say you won't fall into the "nobody wants me" depression on occasion. But this book will show you how to project a positive attitude and effectively use interview follow-up techniques.

You are already a step ahead if you are prepared for the fact that the working world is a far cry from the college campus. What may ease the shock that often accompanies this realization is being forearmed and able to antici-pate a whole new set of rules. This book will give you the lowdown on what to expect and how to handle on-the-job problems.

This manual doesn't stop with the handshake between you and your new employer. It goes on to explain how to cope with the trials and tribulations of your first job and come out a winner.

Trading in your backpack for a briefcase is one of the most difficult transitions you will have to make in your life. It takes years to develop the self-confidence, savvy, and skills you will need to really move ahead. But it's important to start off on the right track; doing well on your first job can be very important to your future career success. You can prepare yourself for what lies ahead and develop a competitive edge if you take to heart some of the ideas offered here.

Note: For simplicity of style and reading, the pronoun "he" is used primarily in the book.

Peggy Schmidt
March 1991

1

Careers

A Job in Your Major: Is It a Prerequisite of
Career Satisfaction? . . . The Right Job: Zeroing
In on Potential Fields of Interest . . . Decision
Making: The Balance-Sheet Approach

Most college students have a severe case of career tunnel vision—they consider seriously only a handful of occupations even though there are 100,000 organizations in this country that employ people in over 20,000 different jobs.

If you are already in a technical curriculum—engineering, computer science, or nursing—you are a step ahead of most people because you have zeroed in on a field, although you still have to decide which particular jobs interest you. But if you are a liberal arts major, you are going to be faced with a double whammy: which field *and* what kind of job are right for you?

Judging from the anxiety level of most seniors when they talk about their future plans, it seems that there are more career identity crises than plans in the making. Even if you have not found a subject you really enjoy or can't see how what you enjoy can be translated into a real job, you should start planning long before graduation. If you don't, you may:

- End up in a profession that your parents have encouraged or even pushed you into, which may not be the one you would choose on your own.

- Decide to look for a job in an area in which you have always done well in school and disregard other equally important factors.

- Look for a job in a field in which you have heard there are plentiful opportunities without stopping to consider whether the job is really right for you.

There is no single reliable indicator of whether a career field is right for you. A career choice should be the result of several different considerations—your interests, values, personality traits, and abilities.

1

Going through a systematic decision-making process requires time and effort, but in the end it can help you avoid dead-ending in the job-market maze.

A Job in Your Major: Is It a Prerequisite of Career Satisfaction?

Almost half of all college graduates do not end up working in fields closely related to their major. I am no exception. I majored in psychology because I found the subject fascinating, rather than because I had a specific career goal in mind. It was not until the middle of my junior year that I realized I wasn't interested in career possibilities in that field. It was too late to switch to a journalism major without putting in an additional year, but my experience as a reporter on the daily newspaper made up what I lacked in formal classroom training. If, like me, you major in social science — psychology, sociology, political science, history, or economics — chances are great (85 percent) that you will not end up working in a field closely related to your major. The accompanying two tables show how much career-potential graduates in various majors felt their first jobs promised and the kinds of jobs graduates in fifteen majors most often land.

The question is: Will you be less satisfied with a job that's not directly related to your major? The answer: No. You *do not* have to use your major in your first job — or your second or third, for that matter — to be content in your work. While salary and status are major influences on career satisfaction, the critical factor is whether you feel you are fully using skills that you may have developed through course work unrelated to your major, extracurricular activities, previous jobs, hobbies, or other personal experience.

There are three reasons why over 20 percent of all college graduates end up in a field unrelated to their major. The first two are voluntary — taking a first job in an unrelated area and becoming interested in the work, or finding a first job in an unrelated field that offers better chances for advancement. The third reason is not being able to find job opportunities in your field.

Studies done by the College Placement Council have found that jobs not requiring a college degree can be just as satisfying to college graduates as traditional ones. Although job status is one of the most important ingredients in career satisfaction, more than four out of ten people who view their jobs as nonprofessional report that they are satisfied with their work. The nonprofessional category includes people in blue-collar and technical jobs, farmers and ranchers, and — in business settings — secretaries, clerks, and administrative assistants. Those in skilled trades are generally more satisfied with their work than are office workers or semiskilled employees.

What kind of person is most likely to find satisfaction in a nonprofessional job? Someone who:

2

- Considers himself popular (he may get satisfaction from good relationships with coworkers or generally have a positive outlook on life).
- Cares about community involvement and achievement (it can be a meaningful substitute for career success).

Who is least likely to find satisfaction in a nonprofessional job? Someone who:

- Is highly creative (he probably has a strong ego and feels overqualified for the job and bored by his responsibilities).
- Has gone to a highly selective college (he may be highly motivated to begin with or simply consider nonprofessional work beneath him).

If your major will not get you far in the job market or you do not mind trading off status for a higher income, a nonprofessional job is worth considering (the skilled trades in particular offer lucrative incomes).

The Right Job: Zeroing In on Potential Fields of Interest

Trying to find the job that will match your interests, skills, and values totally is like finding the perfect relationship — it doesn't exist. As you no doubt have already discovered, trade-offs in life are inevitable. You may come across a career that is a natural for you, only to discover that the best opportunities are in a part of the country you hate. Or you may have to accept a lower-than-ideal salary to buy independence. You should not compromise on the things you feel are important, but you will have to be flexible.

There are several useful ways to get a better idea of whether or not a particular field or job is right for you.

1. *Use a software program.* Your school's career planning and placement office will probably have one of several career assessment software programs. The major ones are:

- DISCOVER from the American College Testing Program
- SIGI PLUS (System of Interactive Guidance and Information — Plus More) from the Educational Testing Service
- Career Navigator from Drake Beam Morin, Inc.
- Career Design Software from Crystal-Barkley Corporation

It's not necessary to know how to use a computer or even how to type in order to use one. These programs are fun because they are interactive. By working through different exercises that help you define your skills, interests, and values, you will get immediate feedback about career choices worth exploring.

2. *Take a vocational interest test.* The two best-known tests are the Strong-Campbell Interest Inventory and the Kuder Occupational

First Jobs of Graduates in 15 Majors

Field of study	% employed in occupations related to field of study	Occupation and % employed in occupation
Nursing	86	Registered nurses (86)
Engineering	78	Engineers (67), engineering technicians and technologists (5), computer specialists (4), graduate student teachers and researchers (2)
Computer and information sciences	75	Programmers (45), computer systems analysts and scientists (20), engineers (7), operations and systems researchers and analysts (2), graduate student teachers and researchers (1)
Accounting	71	Accountants (67), financial managers (4)
Education, except physical education	68	Elementary and secondary school teachers (68)
Mathematics	60	Computer programmers (23), computer systems analysts and scientists (12), elementary and secondary school teachers (10), graduate student teachers and researchers (8), actuaries (5), operations and systems researchers and analysts (1), statisticians (1)
Chemistry	54	Graduate student teachers and researchers (20), chemists (19), chemical technicians (11), chemical engineers (2), secondary school teachers (2)

Physical education	54	Elementary and secondary school teachers (40), college coaches and physical education teachers (7), recreation workers (6), athletes (1)
Art	49	Designers (23), elementary and secondary school teachers (9), painters, sculptors, and artists (8), other artists, performers, and related workers (6), art teachers in colleges and universities (1), drafters (1), photographers (1)
Business and management, except accounting	41	Accountants (8), marketing, advertising, and public relations managers (4), financial managers (2), personnel, training, and labor relations specialists (2), public administration officials (2), management analysts (1), purchasing agents and buyers (1) other managerial occupations (21)
Communications	31	Editors and reporters (11), marketing, advertising, and public relations managers (7), public relations specialists (7), announcers (2), business and promotion agents (2), photographers (2)
Agriculture and natural resources	29	Farm operators and managers (13), science technicians (11), graduate student teachers and researchers (3), forestry and conservation scientists (2)
Home economics	29	Elementary and secondary school teachers (17), dietitians (8), buyers (2), designers (2)
Biological scientists	28	Biological technicians (12), elementary and secondary school teachers (5), biological and life scientists (4), graduate student teachers and researchers (4), chemists (2), forestry and conservation scientists (1)
English	25	Elementary and secondary school teachers (10), editors and reporters (4), technical writers (4), marketing, advertising, and public relations managers (3), graduate student teachers or researchers (2), public relations specialists (2)

Source: Occupational Outlook Quarterly, Summer 1988.

Career Potential of First Jobs by Major

Academic field	Total	Definite career potential	Possible career potential	Temporary until better job found	Temporary until new job starts	Temporary to earn money	Temporary until career decided on	Other
Total, all academic fields	100	41	25	14	2	9	5	4
Accounting	100	46	35	12	1	2	2	2
Agriculture and natural resources	100	43	16	15	2	9	9	6
Art	100	26	28	20	1	17	5	3
Biological sciences	100	22	22	15	1	28	3	9
Business and management, except accounting	100	45	26	15	2	4	5	3
Chemistry	100	32	23	14	3	17	2	9
Communications	100	37	28	19	1	7	5	3
Computer and information science	100	59	23	11	0	4	2	1
Economics	100	49	17	8	1	10	10	5
Education, except physical education	100	40	29	18	2	5	3	3
Engineering	100	56	28	8	0	4	1	3
English	100	27	25	13	1	19	10	9
History	100	34	14	12	3	14	10	13
Home economics	100	40	21	20	0	6	11	2
Mathematics	100	51	17	10	1	12	4	5
Nursing	100	60	27	5	0	5	1	2
Physical education	100	27	26	24	1	9	8	5
Political science	100	27	10	17	2	21	14	9
Psychology	100	23	25	17	1	24	5	5
Sociology	100	27	14	28	0	15	9	7

Source: Occupational Outlook Quarterly, Summer 1988.

Interest Survey. You're asked your preferences in occupations, school subjects, leisure activities, and kinds of people. Your likes and dislikes are then compared with those of professionals working in various fields. The more similar your answers are to those of people in a particular profession, the higher your score for that profession will be. A counselor at your school's career counseling or placement office will help you interpret the results and discuss your questions and reactions. These results are not the final word on which profession you should enter; they're intended to suggest career possibilities and are only a starting point for further research.

3. *Do focused reading.* In each occupation you have listed, there are a number of publications that deal with it exclusively. Many are trade periodicals and newspapers; others are directories and handbooks; a few are nonfiction accounts of what working in that particular field is like. These publications can give you an up-to-date view of trends and job openings and provide a flavor of day-to-day problems and issues. You will probably also get a better idea of the differences among similar jobs you are considering.

Where to Find Business Information by David M. Brownstone and Gordon Carruth has sections that list major newsletters covering business information and trade periodicals. Your career placement office probably won't have current trade periodicals, but your school's business library may. And if your campus is in an urban area, check the newsstands.

Many career planning offices index their information by fields, which makes it easy to do further research. A third source is a professional organization. You can find out names and addresses from your career planning office, or in the *Occupational Outlook Handbook.*

4. *Selectively interview.* If library research is not your forte, or if you're drowning in facts and figures, you can turn to an equally valuable and somewhat less tedious research method — talking with professionals. They can tell you how accurate your perceptions are. If you do that, you'll also be able to get a feeling for whether they're your kind of people, a variable that can influence your choice of a career. After my first summer in New York City, I realized that I fit in with people who were trying to make their living as writers. Of course there were writers whose personalities turned me off and others whose interests were different from mine, but they all shared what to me was the most important quality: an ability to understand one another and feel comfortable in one another's company.

One of the easiest and most acceptable ways of talking with professionals is to attend informal meetings with them that are sponsored by various departments on campus. These sessions are an especially good way of learning how the same job varies depending on the setting, since normally several speakers, each representing a different kind of company, are invited to participate.

If you want a one-to-one conversation, try to arrange interviews with alumni. Before you go, be sure to know what questions you want to ask. Another possibility is simply to call people working in the field that interests you and ask if they would mind spending 15 minutes with you. A professor who teaches a course in that area or your placement director may be able to suggest people to contact.

5. *Meet with a career counselor in your school's career planning and placement office.* The more focused you are when you meet with a career counselor, the better he will be able to help you. Explain the steps you have gone through to come up with your list of career possibilities. If you're not sure how closely any of those occupations matches your values or abilities, ask him for his opinion. The counselor should be able to point out mistaken impressions or oversights and compare your background and academic record with those of students who have made similar career choices.

6. *Work in the field.* Ultimately there is no better way to find out whether you like a job or field than by getting an internship. Keep in mind that you are likely to do beginner's work — don't cross a field off your list simply because you weren't thrilled with its entry-level work. The more important thing is whether you enjoy the feeling of the place and can see yourself doing the work of the more experienced people there. Finally, a word of advice on what are referred to as glamour industries — television, publishing, fashion, movies. Jobs in these fields are often attractive because they are highly visible and provide job status. The myth is that these jobs are more fun than work. The reality is that there is at least as much blood and sweat involved in these jobs as in others. Your chances of getting into a glamour profession are slim because many qualified people compete for the very few jobs. Before you decide to concentrate your studies and job search in a glamour field, make sure that you really would enjoy that work. If you're still attracted, understand what you're up against as well as investigate behind-the-scenes job options in those fields.

Decision Making: The Balance-Sheet Approach

You probably don't have much trouble making up your mind about normal everyday things, but when you're faced with a decision that will have serious consequences in your life, figuring out the best choice can be mind-boggling. Your thoughts may short-circuit, your logic go haywire, and new information not compute. But decision making does not need to be traumatic if you systematically evaluate your options and choose those that make the most sense for you.

People often make big mistakes in the way they make decisions, say psychologists Irving L. Janis and Leon Mann. See if you fit into one of their four categories of decision makers.

Parachuters

These people belong to the jump-before-you-look school. They are likely to say yes to the first thing that looks good, without having researched that option or given any careful consideration to how it stacks up against others. Parachuters may recognize the risks involved in a choice, but they don't view them as serious. Once a Parachuter has zeroed in on a target, he feels committed to jump, even if the conditions change — sometimes with disastrous consequences.

Pretenders

Unlike Parachuters, Pretenders are likely to feel that the risks involved in making a decision are serious, so serious, in fact, that they try to avoid making the decision altogether — even if they know they eventually will have to make a choice. Pretenders act as if life will go on without their having to decide. One of the reasons they can play it so cool is that they daydream about pie-in-the-sky alternatives that have little to do with the choices available to them — making money hustling tennis games or becoming the protégé of a well-known businessman, for example.

Window-jumpers

These are the people who freak out if they feel they are up against the wall — a feeling many college seniors experience the month before graduation. What they hope for is an instant solution that will set them on the right track for the time being — as unlikely as getting an "A" on a test for which they have not studied. A more probable scenario is grabbing any semiviable alternative that happens by (which might be a job in Uncle Louie's flower shop). While there are usually fewer desirable alternatives available to the last-minute decision maker, they still exist — if only he could put aside his anxiety long enough to seek them out.

Coolheads

No matter how crucial a decision is, these people make the smartest choices because they believe they can find a good alternative, even if they are under the same time restrictions as the Window-jumpers. That's because they are able to shelve their emotions and evaluate information that will help them make logical decisions. They realize that even carefully made plans may not work out, sometimes for reasons beyond their control, and have backup choices waiting in the wings.

If your decision-making behavior resembles any of the first three patterns, you can change it. Now is a good time to do that, since taking the Coolhead approach to choosing a career can make the difference of starting out this period of your life on the right foot.

One of the easiest ways to make a decision according to Janis and Mann is to use the balance-sheet approach — listing the advantages and disadvantages of various courses of action. Again, you probably do this in some fashion when you are trying to make a decision. The point is to

Job Comparison Chart

Profession	Education/Experience Required	Income	Work Conditions	Opportunities
Area of specialization	Kind of degree	Starting salary (range)	Fringe benefits	Kinds of organizations hiring college grads
Brief job description	Curriculum requirements	Estimated income after five years' service	Travel possibilities	Areas of country offering job openings
	Prior work experience (co-op, internship, etc.)		Hours (9–5, weekends, etc.)	Outlook for field
	Physical requirements		Physical surroundings	Chances for advancement
			Work effort (on your own, member of department, work for one boss, etc.)	Number of women in field

improve the process by writing down the pros and cons on paper rather than having them float around in your mind.

The information you pick up about career possibilities through reading, interviewing, and work experience can leave your head spinning. One of the easiest ways to synthesize data is to list them in the form of a job comparison chart. Once you have filled in the spaces with the appropriate information, make another chart, using the headings below, and divide it into four sections. Then put each of the factors you have listed on the job comparison chart in one of the sections. You may find that there are as many unappealing things about a career as there are benefits, which is why it is important to assign values to each item in the column. A "1" represents an advantage or disadvantage that is not very important at all, a "5" represents a great deal of importance. If you are considering advertising as a possible career field, your balance sheet might look like this:

Advantages	Rating	Disadvantages	Rating
Good salary	4	Crazy hours — after 5 and on weekends	3
Being able to do creative work	5	Instability — agencies lose accounts and fire employees	2
Working with a lot of fun, zany people	3	Not being able to call any one campaign my own — everything is a team effort	4
Seeing the results of my work	4	A lot of false starts — clients turn down many ideas before selecting one	3
TOTAL	16	TOTAL	12

Even though there are an equal number of advantages and disadvantages, you can see why this career is a sound choice — the Advantage side has more points than the Disadvantage side.

One last factor to consider and to include in your chart is your parents' probable reaction. Their emotional support (and financial support if graduate school is required) may influence your final decision, or the way you decide to implement it.

It also is a good idea to include a column for unknowns that you have no way of knowing until you actually start looking for a job — things beyond your control. If there is not much hiring going on in the field when you graduate, it will be more difficult to find a job. Although it is unreasonable to weigh "what ifs" too heavily in making a decision, if the number or seriousness is high, make a contingency plan.

Considering unknowns also serves another purpose: to insulate you against the pressure you may feel if your original choice meets setbacks and against the "did I do the right thing?" feeling that will haunt you once you finally have arrived at a decision. If you can anticipate what might go wrong, you won't be surprised if it does. Even better, you will be prepared to change plans.

2

A Graduate Degree

A Second Degree: Frill or Investment? . . .
Timing: When to Go to Grad School . . .
Graduate Admission Tests: How to Prepare for
Them . . . Degree Clout: Does Your Alma Mater
Make a Difference? . . . Full-Time or Part-Time
M.B.A.: The Pros and Cons

Record numbers of college graduates are getting second — and even third — degrees. The starting salaries they receive can make graduate school a pretty tempting proposition; those with a master's degree earn about $5,000 a year more than those with only a bachelor's degree. Those with a master's degree in business and engineering earn the highest salaries of all graduates of two-year programs.

A Second Degree: Frill or Investment?

Graduate school is not the answer for everyone, and contrary to what you may hear from your parents or the media, it is not necessary for many professions. The most crucial question is: Is a second degree necessary to get the job *you* want? In some professions — law, medicine, psychology, dentistry, veterinary medicine — the need is obvious. In other fields, whether a graduate degree is necessary for success depends on a great many variables.

The M.B.A. (Master of Business Administration) degree has enjoyed star billing largely because it opens up a wide variety of career options. But that can be a liability as much as an asset. It's true that you do not have to know exactly what you want to do when you apply, but the danger is that you may get a degree in an area of business that simply does not require one.

An M.B.A. is decidedly more useful if you want to get into management in a large corporation than if you plan to work for a small or medium-sized company. The traditional employers of M.B.A.'s are consulting and accounting firms and banks, but an increasing number of graduates are taking manufacturing and marketing positions. M.B.A.'s who want to work in quantitative areas — finance, accounting, operations research — will find the most plentiful job openings. Although an increasing number of business schools are offering courses for entrepreneurs, most people who start their own businesses usually do so without the benefit of a graduate degree, and sometimes without even a college degree.

It makes sense to find out as much as you can about the industry you hope to enter before you enroll in an M.B.A. program. Ask people who have the kind of job you would like and the personnel or college recruitment officers of companies that interest you whether a person with your undergraduate training would benefit from having an M.B.A. in terms of either the type of entry-level job you can land or the salary you can command.

That is likely to be the case if you are a liberal arts major who wants to get into business in certain industries where an M.B.A. can mean being considered for something beyond a secretarial or sales job. Even if on-the-job training is provided, solid business skills are a prerequisite in many fields in order to be hired for the higher-status entry-level positions or management-track jobs. In the automotive industry, for example, beginning jobs in marketing, cost analysis, and planning go to M.B.A.'s.

If you are a woman or a minority group member, a second degree can be a real career booster. The employers' complaint about the lack of "qualified" women and minorities is one that a graduate degree, particularly in business, answers.

Timing: When to Go to Grad School

John O'Hara, a liberal arts graduate, worked as a social worker for four years before he decided to change careers. He went back to school and earned his M.B.A. at age 28. His new profession — metal trading for an international firm — did not require an M.B.A., but John felt that it gave him an understanding of business that he had not developed in his first profession.

Karin McQuillan spent a year in the Peace Corps and three years in magazine and book publishing before she returned to school to get a master's degree in social work. For her, a second degree was an issue of values. Although she was comfortable working in a structured situation, what she enjoyed most was advising people who came to her with problems. She decided to get formal training in psychotherapy and set up her own practice in Boston.

After earning an undergraduate degree in applied math, John McQuillan went on for a master's in computer science, intending to go straight through for his Ph.D. But John began to feel trapped, and he wanted to start making money. He was able to find a job with a small,

14

fast-growing computer company and was able to complete his doctoral thesis, which was closely related to the work he was doing, during his third year on the job.

More and more college seniors are deciding to put off graduate studies for a year or longer because the idea of being in school for another two or three years is a turnoff, or because they want to get some practical experience before committing time or money to a graduate program. If you feel that way or are unsure of what you want to do, it's probably best to hold off. Merely being in a program that will supposedly give you a highly marketable degree won't resolve your uncertainty. Placement officers say that M.B.A. candidates with no work experience often have no better idea of what they want to do than undergraduate students.

In some fields it makes sense to continue your studies without interruption (or with a break of only a year). Law is one. That's because getting ahead in the legal profession usually depends on experience. The older you are when you graduate, the farther behind you will be, because it is virtually impossible to leapfrog your way into a partnership, a corporate position, or even your own practice.

You also might want to think twice about delaying graduate school if you are in a fast-paced field with constant technological and research breakthroughs — computer science, science, and engineering, for example.

But working in the field in which you eventually plan to get an advanced degree can be a good break in your study routine and keep you in touch with new developments.

The biggest advantage of being out in the job market is that you will be able to refine both your career goals and your knowledge of what is required for the job you want. You might find, for example, that you need more management skills if you want to get into an administrative position, or that a promotion to a bottom-line position, with responsibility for major budgetary decisions, may require more technical know-how than you have. Or you may discover that the field you chose is not as satisfying as you thought it would be.

Another consideration is money. A graduate degree can cost anywhere from $10,000 to over $50,000, not including living expenses and wages you would otherwise be earning. If you work for a few years, you may be able to afford the drain more easily or your company might help you out. Many firms offer good tuition aid benefits for employees who earn a degree part-time. Most of those with 500 or more employees do; about half pay full tuition; the rest between 50 and 75 percent.

Delaying graduate study is also a good idea if an advanced degree is not necessary for an entry-level job but is an asset for moving into management.

Business schools, particularly the most prestigious ones, have no objection to a break in your studies. In fact, many admissions officers say they prefer such candidates over those who enter right after graduation.

One reason is that candidates who have worked are often more directed and motivated in their studies; they also get more out of their classes if they have had to deal with real problems similar to those in text-books.

The difference in starting salaries between M.B.A.'s with a few years of work experience and those with none isn't great, but you will probably earn significantly more with an M.B.A. than if you had simply continued working.

The ideal length of time to work before business school is one to five years — not longer. If you are not in the field you want by the time you are 30, you will miss the prime time for putting down roots and developing a good network of contacts. What's more, giving up a job to study for an M.B.A. after you have been out in the work world seven to ten years is not likely to pay off. A *Wall Street Journal* analysis of the cost and return of investing in an M.B.A. found that, even with an above-average starting salary, the investment would not be earned back without superstar raises (assuming the M.B.A. student had ten years' working experience and quit a job paying $50,000). And since you probably will have a close relationship or family commitments by then, you run a greater risk of encountering conflicts between your career and personal life.

Graduate Admission Tests: How to Prepare for Them

The two most heavily weighed factors in graduate school admissions are your undergraduate grade point average and your scores on standardized admission tests. You're likely to do best if you take the test during your junior or senior year of college because that's when you're in test-taking shape and course material is fresh in your mind. If, however, you have been out of school for a year or more, your test-taking skills will probably be rusty and your ability to recall details won't be as sharp.

In either case, you can improve your scores by practicing your test-taking techniques and reviewing some subject areas. With the exception of the special subject tests that are an optional feature of the Graduate Record Exams, admission tests are aptitude tests. Their purpose is to measure skills and knowledge developed over an entire academic career, rather than knowledge of specific subjects. But several factors can influence how well you do— familiarity with test directions, the concepts behind test questions, and how they are phrased. If you learn to pace yourself by taking practice tests under conditions similar to actual ones, you also can boost your score.

What about a formal test preparation course? Some are offered by big operations like Stanley H. Kaplan Educational Center, Inc. There is no statistical evidence that students who take these courses score significantly higher than they would have without such preparation. The Educational Testing Service, which designs the Law School Admission Test (LSAT) and the Graduate Management Admission Test (GMAT) among others, claims that coaching will improve your scores only if you have had no formal course work in math immediately prior to taking an admission exam.

Many students, however, swear by these courses.

Their format usually includes a lecture by an instructor (he may be a graduate student who took the test recently or a professor) followed by a practice test and an explanation of the correct answers. (These practice tests do not contain questions from actual admission tests but are designed to cover the tested concepts.) Since the lectures provide only a review of the subject, you will not learn enough from them to do well if you have not taken a formal course previously.

Courses that meet for up to 32 hours of class time can cost as much as $700. If you do not feel disciplined enough to study on your own or if you have been out of school a long time and feel that a structured course would help build your confidence, it may be a worthwhile investment. Keep in mind that you will get more from a course that meets over several weeks' time than from a one-shot cram course and that you can't ask questions in a videotape course.

Be sure to find out what the tuition for the course covers. Sometimes additional library tapes that cover subject areas in greater depth, additional question-and-answer sessions with instructors, or study-at-home workbooks are offered. You can find test-preparation courses under that heading in the yellow pages.

If you decide to study on your own, you can use the full-length sample tests provided in the test-information bulletin you receive when you register for a test. Or you can buy one of the many review books available. Go through a table of contents to make sure the one you buy includes good review sections for the subjects in which you need the most help.

Study experts say you can get just as much from a review book as you can from a course if you have good study habits. Time yourself on practice tests to develop your pacing. One of the best ways to learn material is to take a section of the test and correct it to see what your mistakes were. Find out why you answered a question incorrectly. Some review books give explanations for certain sections; others do not; you may have to ask a professor or graduate student for help. Be sure to familiarize yourself with the test directions and time limits for the various sections of the test. Those included in sample tests designed by the testing agency generally are the same directions that will appear on the actual test. Misreading the directions can lose you points; having to reread directions during the test session costs you time.

You may also be able to pick up useful test-taking techniques at your school's study and learning skills center. It is a good idea to start reviewing and taking practice tests at least two months before the test.

Degree Clout: Does Your Alma Mater Make a Difference?

In a word, yes. But that does not mean a top-name school is your best bet. A lot depends on the kind of firm you want to work for and where the opportunities in your field can be found.

If you're after a Fortune 500 company or a highly respected law firm, you'll do much better with a degree from a prestigious school. That's where corporate giants and top-name law firms do their head-hunting. They spare no expense in impressing prospective employees with salary benefits and their own prestige. (As the only firms that can afford to recruit across the country, these companies often expect you to relocate.)

Another advantage of a name school is its alumni network. You can bank on your alma mater as a golden password in getting interviews.

You can get away with going to a good graduate school that does not have a national reputation if you are more interested in working for a less prestigious or smaller firm in the city where you live or went to school. Such a company usually cares more about finding good students who know the area and plan to stay. As long as you have a respectable academic record and fit their job requirements, you stand a good chance of getting hired.

Top firms generally are image-conscious. That means they may prefer people who talk a certain way (and have—or do not have, as the case may be—a particular accent), who dress in the style of the organization (often Brooks Brothers conservative), and who know the same people (that's why one's alma mater often counts more than one's grades).

If you're concerned about whether a degree from a particular school is worth the time and money, ask its placement director where its graduates have gotten jobs. Business and law schools usually keep the most thorough placement records — they can tell you the fields their graduates go into, the cities they work in, their starting salaries, and how long it took them to get their jobs. Another possibility is to check with the personnel office of employers in whom you are interested to find out if they have hired graduates from schools you are considering.

Full-Time or Part-Time M.B.A.: The Pros and Cons

More and more graduate students are going part-time—a choice influenced by their particular field, the cost of tuition, and their amount of free time.

Even if you want to begin graduate school right after college, you still have a choice to make.

The Advantages of Going Full-Time

1. *The value of a one-track mind.* Not having to split your time and loyalty between course work and job responsibilities usually makes

learning easier. You are more likely to become immersed in what you are doing when you spend a major portion of your day thinking and talking about, and preparing for, the subjects you are studying. And directing your energy totally into your studies can make it easier to see relationships among the different courses you are taking: you may understand the whole picture more quickly.

If you have little formal preparation in the field in which you are getting your degree, that may be especially important.

2. *Better chance to develop future contacts.* There's good reason beyond mutual moral support and academic help to get to know your fellow students. Like professors, they're important contacts for the future. Inside information about jobs and job offers is exchanged among people who "did time" together in college and graduate school. Full-time students generally spend more time with professors and other students.

3. *Faster route to a degree.* Time is money, and there is no doubt that although you may have to cut corners while you are in school, you will start earning a higher income years before your part-time counterpart.

The Disadvantages of Going Full-Time

1. *Deferring your entry into the real world.* The idea of extending your student life and identity may be a turnoff, but you may be able to satisfy your itch to get into the working world by using the credential of a year of graduate studies to get a summer or part-time job in your field.

2. *Living a penny-pinching life-style.* The bad news is that graduate school may make an even bigger dent in your wallet (or your parents' wallet) than your undergraduate studies did. The good news is there is loan money available. Many more full-time than part-time students are eligible for federal grants and loans. (You must be enrolled half-time — usually 6 credit hours — to apply for most federal grants and loans.) A full-time student stands a much better chance of getting loans and grants simply because he has little if any current income. Full-time students also have the option of paying for tuition with research or teaching assistantships, many of which include a stipend that helps subsidize living expenses. Assistantships are less prevalent in business or law school. If you are a full-time M.B.A. candidate, one thought that should console you is that the lifetime earnings of M.B.A.'s who pursued their degrees full-time is slightly higher than that of those who did it on a part-time basis.

The Advantages of Going Part-Time

1. *Getting a free or a subsidized ride from your employer.* You may not have to pay any tuition costs, or only part of them, if you decide to get your degree part-time. Most large companies offer employees some kind of tuition assistance. The only catch is that your courses must be job-related or prepare you for a job within your company — most employers are not eager to help you change your career.

Firms most likely to have tuition-aid programs are those in the manufacturing, transportation, communications, utilities, finance, and insurance fields. Wholesale and retail businesses are less likely.

2. *Taking classes with other working people.* Taking courses in the evening offers several advantages. First, the professor is more likely to gear out-of-class assignments to the schedules of students who are working full-time. That doesn't mean you necessarily will get away with less work, but there probably will be more flexibility in deadlines for assignments. Second, your professor is likely to be agreeable to your making up missed assignments or tests if the demands of your job keep you from class. Finally, although you will not get to know as many students in a part-time program because you are not all moving through at the same pace, the contacts you do make are likely to have a more immediate impact on your career since they — and you — have a good line on current job-opening information.

Disadvantages of a Part-Time Degree

1. *Not being able to attend a top-name school.* The most prestigious law and business schools offer only full-time daytime schedules for students. But an increasing number of more-than-adequate graduate schools, particularly urban ones, are adding part-time programs to accommodate the changing needs of prospective students.

2. *Taking a longer time to complete your degree.* While a part-time degree may be more cost-effective, it undoubtedly will retard your progress or delay your entry into a new field. One compromise is to go part-time for two or three years and then take off one academic year to complete your course work. That way, you only have to worry about nine months without an income and you will be in the job market sooner. If you can grow in your present job, you don't need to be so concerned about time — usually three to five years for a two-year full-time program (assuming you take at least two courses each term).

3. *Losing some of your free time.* Probably the toughest thing about the full-time job/part-time school routine is that you have less time to spend with your family and friends or to participate in leisure or community activities. Chances are you will spend two full evenings or more a week in class, depending on how many courses you take. And you can count on spending 2 to 4 hours more preparing for each hour of class time, which no doubt will cut into your weekends. On the other hand, if you are the kind of person who tends to do more constructive things with time if it is structured and work is expected of you, you may enjoy the discipline of a part-time program; your degree may contribute to your sense of accomplishment as well as your overall career plans.

3

Employers

Whom to Work For: The Government, a Nonprofit Organization, or Private Industry . . . Fortune 500 or Small Business: What Size Company Best Suits Your Personality? . . . Where to Look for Work: Hometown, College Town, or New City . . . Working for Your Family's Business: Asset or Liability? . . . On Your Own: Can You Pay the Rent If You Are Self-Employed? . . . Working Abroad: How Feasible a Career Plan?

For five months between my first and second jobs, I worked as a temporary in a succession of offices. At the time, the only merit I could see in that was a regular paycheck. But being older and wiser than I was at 22, I now recognize the advantage of having observed firsthand just about every kind of office there is. I worked in a large corporation's executive suite whose sereneness I found downright spooky, a busybody office where some people knew more about my personal life than I did, and a paternalistic company where employees got orchids from the personnel department on their first anniversary of employment. My office-jumping experience may be one of the reasons why I stayed with one magazine for almost eight years—I recognized a good thing when I had it.

Whether your personality is simpatico with your employer's has a major effect on how satisfied you'll be with your job. Instead of letting an interviewer decide whether you'll fit in at the company, turn the tables. Analyze which employers are right for you before you choose your interviews.

Whom to Work For: The Government, a Nonprofit Organization, or Private Industry

Working for the government no more makes you a drone than working for a nonprofit organization makes you a do-gooder or working for private industry makes you a moneygrubber. But there are real differences among these three sectors. College graduates who work in private industry claim to be the most satisfied, but that varies depending on occupational group.

Here are some of the major differences.

The Federal Government

Which agency you work for is not as important as what you do on the job—there's no glamour being a minor paper-pusher in a prestigious agency. The best way to beat the bureaucracy is to work in a field office (outside of D.C.), where the staffs usually are smaller and more autonomous.

Responsibility. If you are bright and determined, you can have more responsibility at a younger age than in industry. Because small decisions here often have a big impact, there are plenty of opportunities to make your opinion count. *If* you prove yourself.

Raises. Annual step increases (there are ten "steps" within each GS level) are given to those who turn in at least a satisfactory performance. But for recent college grads who perform well, promotion to the next grade level (there are fifteen grades) is common within the first eighteen months on the job.

Promotion. Job levels are well-defined, and the entry-level employee who proves himself can move up relatively quickly; the system, however, can stymie the ambitious employee on a higher level.

Security. Firing is rare, and while the government is vulnerable to downsizing due to political or economic changes, employees are usually relocated or reassigned rather than given a pink slip.

Benefits. Only some big corporations offer better fringe benefits.

Note: Working for your state or local government can be an entirely different story. The salaries are lower, and there is more instability since their budgets are subject to the whims of the voters.

Private Industry

Well, folks, this is the long run, the place to make big bucks. Success here is what the American Dream is all about. But be prepared to put in long hours—that's the biggest price of success in this sector.

Responsibility. As a rule, the smaller the employer, the more you will take on, and the sooner.

Raises. Almost always given on merit. Performance standards are relatively clear-cut in big corporations but can be downright arbitrary there on out. Cost-of-living increases are rare.

Promotion. Unless you're working for a small and fast-growing company, moving up is tougher than in government. There are many more greenhorns hacking their way through the entry-level job jungle.

Security. Employees no longer feel that loyalty and productivity automatically mean their job is protected. The bottom line is that unless you have an employment contract (few entry-level employees can get one), a union contract, or a wonderful employee handbook (that says that employees can be fired only for good cause or for specific reasons listed in it), you can be fired at your employer's whim—and have no legal recourse.

Benefits. They range from excellent (big corporations) to nonexistent (small employers with shoestring operations). It pays to examine carefully the benefits of an employer who falls between the two before you accept a job.

Nonprofit Organizations

Some nonprofit organizations offer opportunities comparable to those in private industry. Few are so big that you cannot see the results of your work. That, in fact, is one of the big pluses of the nonprofit sector. So if psychic income means more to you than a fat paycheck, you'll fit in with this crowd.

Responsibility. Requires a lot of personal initiative. Since many nonprofit organizations are top-heavy with experienced staff, you may have to work your tail off to convince them that you are capable of taking on responsibility.

Raises. Usually based on merit. Performance standards are even more subjective than those in private industry. With profit not a goal, everyone's work is less quantifiable. Personality can play an important role here.

Promotion. As in private industry, moving up often depends on the size of the organization. If you are competitive and willing to work hard, you have an advantage over the majority of your peers, who are more interested in making a contribution than a name for themselves.

Security. Somewhat less stable than government, but more secure than in private industry. Firing is rare; layoffs are often tied to cuts in funding.

Benefits. Vacation time is usually more generous than in private industry or government, but other benefits on the whole are less comprehensive than those of the other two groups because there is simply less money to go around.

Fortune 500 or Small Business: What Size Company Best Suits Your Personality?

Working in a huge corporation is something like going to a giant state university; if you don't find your own "corner," you feel like a cog in the wheel. Conversely, a "ma and pa" type business is something like a very small college; you can't help getting caught up in the spirit of the place.

Most companies fall in between. Where you'll be most comfortable depends on the job itself and on your personality.

Surveys show that people who work for small companies are more satisfied than those who work for large ones but that both are happier than people who work in medium-sized companies (100 to 500 employees). One reason for the seeming discrepancy is that people in large companies often work in small departments that function, for all practical purposes, like small businesses.

People in nonprofessional jobs place more importance on working for a small company than do professionals. All three types have pros and cons.

The Corporate Environment

First, the good news: Large corporations (over 500 employees) offer the best salaries and opportunity to move up. Employees are reviewed regularly, and standards of performance are determined by the company rather than by individual bosses. Because of their extensive in-house training programs, corporations are a great place to nail down a solid few years of experience. Working for a big company also gives you instant recognition outside your firm, which can greatly ease getting business done.

Large corporations have other advantages: If you find you're not getting ahead in one department or have problems with your boss, you usually can transfer to another department if you're performing well. Procedures for making complaints, if you think you've been treated unfairly or aren't getting deserved assignments or promotions, are formalized. The fringe benefits are tops—health coverage plans are comprehensive; tuition-aid plans are common; stock benefits or profit-sharing plans often are available to employees. Well-staffed support services often mean less drudgery for you. And the research, testing, and library services can provide valuable information that will help you in your work.

Now the bad news: The red tape involved in getting approval, decisions, or feedback can be exasperating. There's pressure on you to plan ahead so that your work isn't held up because the "powers that be" can't get back to you immediately.

Jobs are much more highly specialized in a large company, and that means fewer opportunities to do things outside your prescribed responsibilities. Dabbling is difficult because people are territorial about their jobs. While dress codes are pretty much a thing of the past, individuality is usually frowned upon because it doesn't usually fit in with the "uniform" image of the company. And at some companies people even address one another by their last names.

In most large companies, you probably can get away with working less hard and not having that noticed (on the other hand, your contributions attract less attention, too). You can put in a scant nine-to-five day and still be considered an ambitious employee if you produce while you are there.

The Small Office

Any business that has fewer than twenty employees is, for the purpose of this chapter, a small office. Between 1978 and 1982, small offices created 40 percent of all new jobs. That trend is expected to continue in the future because service industries will grow faster than manufacturing, and service work sites tend to have fewer employees than do those where goods are produced.

Probably the biggest advantage of working for a small firm is that you can see the effect of your daily contributions. Small businesses have a familylike ambiance — everyone has to cooperate or things just don't get done. If you have a problem or question, you probably can walk straight into the boss's office and get it cleared up.

Another big plus is the chance to get involved in learning the whole business. You'll still have your own responsibilities, but if someone is short-handed, yours may well be the extra pair. You sometimes may feel that you're in over your head, but if you do a passable job, your boss will develop confidence in you.

There are down sides of working for a small business, too. Moving up is more difficult because there are fewer positions to move to; unless the company is a fast-growing one, you'll have to wait until someone moves out. And if you're not getting along with your boss, your only alternative is to leave.

Because of the close quarters, personality conflicts are common; if you learned to coexist with a roommate who drove you crazy, you will no doubt be able to tolerate wacko coworkers. Since the structure of the organization often is not well defined, you may have problems with a coworker about who is responsible for a given task. The stronger personality often wins.

You will have to work harder in a small company — and both your mistakes and accomplishments will be more visible. If the company is expanding quickly, the possibility of taking on a major role at a young age — and the salary to match it — are excellent. While there are no formal training programs, the opportunities for on-the-job training are often great, especially if you take the initiative.

You will have a more personal relationship with your boss and coworkers, but you may have less privacy. Small offices can be like soap operas. If you're on good terms with most of your colleagues, that won't be a problem. If not, the closeness may be claustrophobic.

Medium-sized companies of 100 to 500 employees share more of the characteristics of big corporations; those with 25 to 100 employees more nearly resemble small businesses.

Many typical summer jobs are informal outdoor or service jobs in restaurants and hotels where size doesn't much affect your job satisfaction. That's why it's useful to work as an intern or in a part-time or summer job in your field to give you a flavor of the differences among businesses of various sizes.

Where to Look for Work: Hometown, College Town, or New City?

Where you look for work will determine how soon you'll get a job and how quickly you'll adjust, so a little geographic soul-searching is needed before you begin researching or interviewing.

Three key things to consider:

- Do you want the experience of living in a new area?
- Would you be willing to relocate if you were offered the right job?
- Are most of the opportunities in your field clustered in a few areas of the country?

Here are the three most common options — hometown, college town, and new city — and the experiences of college graduates who tried each.

Hometown Jobs

Finding a first job often is easiest in your hometown or nearby. You're familiar with the employers there, and many of the people with hiring power know, or know about, you or your family. If you stayed near home for college you have the best set of contacts imaginable.

Lucy Flynn started building a career in politics and government in her hometown of Framingham, Massachusetts, when she ran at the age of 18 for the Democratic Town Committee. In her freshman and senior years at a nearby college, she interned for a city council member. That led to her first job as his administrative assistant. At 26, Lucy was appointed state coordinator of the New England Regional Commission, an agency that handles transportation, economic development, and energy issues.

A job in your hometown also can make the transition from student to employee less painful. With no need to deal with the hassles of getting established in new surroundings, and a built-in social life, you can focus your attention almost exclusively on your job. Since many first jobs do not pay terrific salaries, you can afford to live comfortably because a hometown job gives you the option of "crashing" with Mom and Dad until you can save enough to move into respectable quarters of your own.

Probably the major drawback of working in your hometown, unless it's in a major metropolitan area, is the lack of job options.

26

College-Area Opportunities

Unless you've led an ivory-tower existence for four years, your chances of landing a job probably are very good. College contacts are even more likely than hometown employers to be familiar with your recent accomplishments and employment track record. John McQuillan had no trouble finding his first job at a small computer company near his college. Not only is Cambridge, Massachusetts, a technology center, but several of John's friends were working there and were able to recommend him.

If your college town or city does not support much business or industry in your field, you lose much of your built-in advantage, especially if the area is a popular one for college students and recent grads.

Employment in a New City or Area

This option is hands down the most difficult for several reasons:

- You have the fewest contacts, and that may mean a protracted job search.
- Even if you plan to line up a job before you relocate, a long job search that includes travel can be expensive.
- If you relocate first and then look for a job, you will have to deal with the ups and downs of a job search with no family or friends for support.
- If the area is very different from your home or college town, you may develop a case of culture shock severe enough to make you want to head home within a few months.

But looking for a job in a new area of the country can be the best move you ever made *if* that is where the best job opportunities in your field are. If you have always dreamed about living somewhere else, now when you have no financial and family commitments is the best time of your life to make the move.

The summer after my junior year of college, I packed my bags and left my home state, Ohio, for a three-month stay in New York City, a place I had been to only once before, when I was 12. I knew no one there, but I had read plenty of books set in New York, and it seemed like a writer's heaven. I wanted to find out firsthand what it would be like to live there. I took graduate courses at Columbia University and worked full-time as a secretary in an East Village art gallery. I met plenty of struggling writers, and I even met some established writers I never dreamed I would ever get a chance to talk to—among them Tennessee Williams and Elia Kazan. That summer was crucial to my career plans: it helped me see what things were important in a job, and it crystalized my idea of where I could fit in in the writing world. While none of the people I met that summer proved to be great job contacts, when I returned seven months later, I had friends who gave me emotional support and places to stay during my job search.

If you do not have any job contacts in the area, check with your alumni office or that city's alumni group, or participate in a university-sponsored summer institute or seminar. They offer good opportunities to meet people with similar interests and professionals working in the field. New York University, for example, runs a publishing institute annually.

If you are considering moving to a new area, be sure to check out two helpful guides: *Places Rated Almanac* by Richard Boyer and David Savagean and *Finding Your Best Place to Live in America* by Dr. Thomas F. Bowman, Dr. George A. Guiliani, and Dr. M. Ronald Minge.

Working for Your Family's Business: Asset or Liability?

Working for your parents or close relatives can be an ideal first job or a nightmare. If your career interests are strong and would not be furthered by working in your family's business, you will be better off holding out even though working for your family seems like an oasis in the desert. If you're undecided about your career, working for your family's business can do one of several things:

- Show you that if you're given some responsibility, you might enjoy the work more than you did when you were working summers or part-time.
- Extend your state of career limbo because you will not be exposed to different career opportunities.
- Convince you that you would go crazy if your family's business were the main focus in your life.

A family business large enough to offer you an opportunity to pursue interests you have developed on your own is the best. But even that arrangement will work much better if you know what you want before you make a commitment.

Androc Kislevitz went through three jobs and a graduate degree in advertising before he decided to join his father's business, a toy company that employed 145 people.

For the first six months, Andy was a handyman—he did jobs no one else wanted—to learn the business from the bottom up and to play down the fact that he was the boss's son. The marketing/sales manager left to join another company six months after Andy arrived, and Andy took over. At first, he made a lot of mistakes since the only thing he knew about media buying was what he had learned in a course, but he was allowed to grow into the job. Andy's career zoomed in the next five years, and he became marketing/sales manager.

Working in a family business his first year out of college gave Gary Ryan time to think about what he wanted to do next—something he had not seriously considered in college—while providing a weekly pay-check. He knew that he did not want to take on a permanent role in the business, and his family did not pressure him to do so. Gary used the money he saved by living at home to pay for a two-year M.B.A. program. After he graduated, he went to work for a Big Eight accounting firm.

Pluses and Minuses of Working in Your Family's Business

Before you make up your mind about working for your family's business, weigh the advantages and disadvantages.

Advantages

- Being given a great deal of responsibility relative to experience
- Earning a better salary than your counterparts in similar jobs elsewhere (if the business is profitable)
- Getting an inside look at how a business runs — you will be privy to information usually available only to management or owners
- Moving up quickly into a job and title because of your unique relationship with the owner
- Having your ideas listened to and implemented if they are sound — a phenomenon unheard of among most people in first jobs
- Getting experience managing other people
- Being exposed to decision making and working with key people in the company

Disadvantages

- Suffering from the "boss's son" syndrome — resentment from older and more experienced employees as well as your peers is common because of your privileged position
- Being caught in the middle when you discover a problem or inefficiency. Do you bring it to your parent's attention and jeopardize the trust of the employee responsible or let it surface on its own?
- Not being a part of the office grapevine or social groups unless people want something from you
- Being expected to put in long hours when necessary
- Making an adjustment, possibly to a less prestigious or responsible job, if you decide to leave the family business

The benefits and problems are somewhat different if you work for a small family business where most of the key people — or all the employees — are members of your immediate family. While the job may provide security and a good salary, there will probably be fewer opportunities to manage others and play a key role yourself because of competition from other family members. One big problem is the family business squabble that comes up when areas of responsibilities are not well-defined, or when one person has ultimate decision-making power. You also may find that you do not perform at your peak level because the family's expectations are not so high or well shaped as an outside employer's would be.

On Your Own: Can You Pay the Rent If You Are Self-Employed?

You would like nothing better than to be your own boss. You may have an idea for a product or service that no one else offers. Or you want to sell your work on a free-lance basis.

The benefits of self-employment are tremendous; college students felt that the opportunities to get ahead in a business of their own were as good as, if not better than, in a large corporation, and were considerably better in the former than if they worked in a small business, a government agency, or a nonprofit organization. But the risk of failure, especially right out of college, is high. Why is the going so tough? The major problem is lack of experience. Unless you learn the ins and outs of the same or a similar business through summer or part-time employment, you're bound to make mistakes the hard way. Mistakes can be expensive and can even cause you to lose your shirt. If you haven't worked in the business before, your hunch about the "uniqueness" or feasibility of your entrepreneurial scheme may be off-base, too. You don't have a good enough feel for the marketplace to be aware of the pitfalls of your plan.

The second problem is commitment. You have to be very sure this is how you want to spend the next several years — and few college seniors know themselves that well. Unlike a first job, your own business or free-lance work is not necessarily a stepping-stone to a better position, it's more an end in itself: the business has to grow for you to move ahead.

The third problem is that most people who go into business for themselves underestimate their turnaround time — how much money they will have to invest before they begin to show a profit. More than half of all small businesses fail within the first five years. That's what happened to Charles Wilson, who worked as a newspaper reporter for two years before he cofounded a small weekly newspaper. Even though the paper was popular with readers, he and his partner ran out of capital after a year. Charles decided to get an M.B.A. to develop a better background in budgeting and cost analysis.

Going it alone is decidedly tougher than getting a first job, and a venture is destined to sputter unless you have abundant amounts of enthusiasm, patience, money, and foresight. The most promising business for recent grads to start is one aimed at the student market, the market with which they're most familiar. Knowing what's already available and what is needed and how much the buyer is willing to spend is crucial to success.

If you are determined to give your idea a try, be sure to do the following before you invest much money:

1. *Know your product.* Investigate its range of usefulness. Make sure you understand good and poor quality. Check out the competition.

2. *Do market research.* Find out if your hunches about potential con-

sumers are on target. Investigate ways to sell, distribute, and promote your product.

3. *Calculate your risk.* How much of an initial investment will be necessary? What will your overhead be? How long will it take before you see a return on your investment?

4. *Decide how much time and effort your business will require.* Figure out whether you can handle your business alone or will need someone with expertise you don't have to make it work. Will that person be a partner or employee? If it's at all possible, get a full- or part-time job and moonlight your business until you find out whether you have got what it takes to become a successful entrepreneur.

There are also some excellent books available on setting up your own business. Some of them are:

- *The Entrepreneur's Manual: Business Start-Up, Spin-Offs and Innovative Management,* by Richard M. White (Chilton Book Co.)

- *The Field Guide to Starting a Business,* by Stephen M. Pollan and Mark Levine (Fireside Books)

- *So You've Got a Great Idea,* by Steve Fiffer (Addison-Wesley)

- *Growing a Business,* by Paul Hawken (Fireside Books)

Working Abroad: How Feasible a Career Plan?

If you have traveled or studied in a foreign country and have fallen in love with the idea of living abroad, you might want to join the million Americans who live and work overseas. Finding a job abroad is not easy, however, because many countries place restrictions on hiring foreigners. Still, the job market for Americans has been expanding because the dollar has been weaker and the demand for U.S. goods and services strong, according to Will Cantrell, editor of a monthly newsletter called *The International Employment Hotline.*

There are many ways into the international job market, but if you are serious about cracking it, keep the following things in mind:

- Fluency in a foreign language is not a prerequisite for many jobs, although it can give you an edge and in some countries is essential to getting around on your own outside the American community you are living or working in.

- Your pay will probably be equal to, if not higher than, what you would make in the United States, but keep in mind that the cost of living in some countries may be higher than what you are accustomed to.

- Europe is often the top choice of would-be American expatriates, but unless you work for the Department of Defense, which maintains many military bases there, you will have a difficult time finding work. Unemployment is high in some countries, and job seekers from European Community countries are favored.

The best job prospects abroad are for educators, particularly those with state certification, two years' recent teaching experience, and a bachelor's degree in the field in which they are teaching. Elementary, secondary, and vocational school teachers are regularly hired by Defense Department–dependent schools, international schools supported by the diplomatic community, private schools catering to English-speaking students, and even public schools and universities.

The biggest employer of Americans overseas is the U.S. government. The armed forces sends the largest number of employees, both military and civilian, overseas. People in a wide variety of occupations including recreational and sports specialists, social workers, nurses, psychologists, and medical therapists are needed on military bases, according to Judy McArdle, president of Federal Research Service, Inc.

The Departments of Agriculture, Commerce, and Transportation also hire personnel for overseas assignments, but they usually want people with special skills — in agriculture, civil engineering, architecture, and planning and accounting. The most glamorous overseas government jobs are with the foreign service branch of the Department of State. But jobs in one of the more than 300 foreign embassies require passing rigorous written and oral exams.

If being a part of the American military does not appeal to you and you do not have specific skills to offer to the other branches, another alternative is the Peace Corps, which operates in over sixty countries. The countries with the largest programs are Kenya, Honduras, Guatemala, Morocco, Botswana, and Jamaica. More than half of the Peace Corps volunteers do their stints in Africa. Placements in Eastern Europe are growing, too. You are given a living allowance, and a monthly salary is set aside for you to collect once you complete two years of service. Since you will be in a developing country, the savings opportunities will be great.

Many students look for jobs with multinational corporations with the idea of applying for an overseas position once in. But the number of American corporate personnel working in company branches overseas is minuscule, mainly because U.S. employers can bring in U.S. citizens only if there are no nationals qualified to do the job. The only people who are assigned overseas then are those with specialized skills. This usually means persons with extensive experience working in their area and usually with a proven track record with the company. Another problem is the cost of maintaining American employees overseas.

The third big overseas employer is the international nonprofit agency. Most of the 400 such U.S. organizations have programs in developing countries. These jobs do not offer good salaries. Your reward will be derived almost exclusively from satisfaction with your work.

Another option is to work as a legal au pair through an approved program such as the American Institute for Foreign Study's (AIFS) Family Helper in Europe. It's a good way to perfect your language skills, find out if you like living abroad, and investigate other job opportunities. For more information, write: AIFS, 102 Greenwich Avenue, Greenwich, CT 06830.

Even if you find a job abroad, your experience may not help you get a better job once you return to the United States. Anita Cotter was luckier than most liberal arts graduates looking for a job in Europe. She was fluent in French and German and found a job as a research assistant in a brokerage house in West Germany. She spent two years working there and traveled through Europe on weekends and vacations. Then she moved to Paris, where she taught English to French businessmen. But when she finally returned to the United States after three years abroad, she had to start out in an entry-level position to get her foot into the publishing world.

If you feel sufficiently discouraged about overseas job prospects but still want to see the world, consider this idea: work for an American company in this country (even a small one) that has one or more offices overseas. While you probably will not be able to travel on international business right away, you can work your way into a position of responsibility and eventually be assigned to go on business trips. Tom Kemp got his first job with a San Francisco–based publishing company that has offices in London, Brussels, and Tokyo. He was sent on his first business trip abroad after a year on the job. In five years, his business trips averaged two a year; he usually adds a week's vacation time.

John O'Hara had similar opportunities in his work with metal trading companies, most of which transact international business. In five years John traveled on business to China, Europe, and South America.

Virginia Kamsky, who once worked in the international division of a major bank, spends several months of the year in China. Two years after she completed graduate work in Chinese and economics, the United States resumed diplomatic relations with China. Since there were few people at the bank with her background and facility with the language, she was given major responsibilities. She now runs her own consulting business and advises U.S. clients on how to do business in China.

Employment agencies that tout overseas vacancies do not always operate in the interests of their clients. Several are under investigation by the attorneys general of the states in which they operate.

Before you pay an agency to help you find a job, ask (1) what the fee is, who pays it (usually the employer), and when; (2) how their matchup process works; (3) how they collect information about job vacancies; and (4) whether they have recently placed job hunters with your experience and skills. Asking for the names of satisfied clients is another way to determine if the agency is reputable and successful.

The following publications can be helpful in finding a job abroad:

- *Federal Career Opportunities,* biweekly listing of domestic and overseas federal job vacancies (Federal Research Service, Inc., P.O. Box 1059, Vienna, VA 22183-1059)

- *International Employment Hotline,* monthly newsletter (Cantrell Corporation, P.O. Box 3030, Oakton, VA 22124)
- *The ISS Directory of Overseas Schools,* annual guide to elementary and secondary schools in foreign lands (International Schools Services)
- *Making It Abroad: The International Job Hunting Guide,* by Howard Schuman (John Wiley & Sons)

4

The Job Campaign

Resumes and Cover Letters: How to Make Yours Stand Out . . . On-Campus Recruitment: Are Assembly-Line Interviews Worthwhile? . . . The Self-Initiated Search: Stalking the Elusive Job Opening . . . Contacts: The Who-You-Know Strategy Works . . . Job Fairs: The Smorgasbord Approach to Meeting Employers . . . Employment Agencies: Are They Looking Out for You or Trying to Make a Fast Buck? . . . Help-Wanted Ads: Stacked Deck? . . . Government Jobs: How to Apply to the Country's Biggest Employer

The worst part about getting your first job is having to go out and look for it. Rejection is built into the system, and even if you know it has nothing to do with you personally, it is hard to keep your ego intact when people repeatedly tell you no.

My first job campaign was nothing short of an unmitigated disaster, at least when it came to strategy. My aim was to find a writing job at a newspaper, magazine, television station, or radio station (a lofty ambition for a graduate whose only experience was on the school newspaper).

I began my job search by digging through the *New York Times* classifieds. I sent in fifty resumes for jobs that promised challenge, travel, and glamour and received two letters asking me to come in for interviews — one was from a sex magazine. I went out of curiosity and was offered the job, which I declined. I simply couldn't imagine myself on the magazine's softball team wearing a T-shirt emblazoned with its logo. The other was from a fly-by-night newsletter whose publisher was notorious for his hare-brain publishing tactics, which included spending what should have been his staff's salaries on expensive advertisements for his newsletter.

Visiting employment agencies was my next step. The less-good agencies made me feel they were doing me a favor when they sent me off to insurance companies and brokerage houses, places where I would not have considered working on an in-house publication let alone in some other position. The better agencies — those that specialized in media placement — sent me to places I liked that offered me jobs I didn't want. My one attempt at a direct onslaught was at the *New York Times:* the personnel officer told me that the best I could hope for was a secretarial slot, and there was a long waiting list for even that.

How did I get my first job? Through a contact I made when I was looking for an apartment. The tenant who was leaving mentioned she had recently quit her job at a major women's magazine and suggested I apply for it. I did not have the basic good sense to ask her what the job was or who her boss was — I just arrived at the offices of the personnel department the next Monday morning and asked for a job interview. I was offered a job as an editorial assistant a week later.

I used to think that I landed my first job because I was lucky; but I have since learned that luck implies more than most people think it does — luck is the intersection of ambition and opportunity. In job boom times (which prevailed when I graduated) luck comes more readily. In a competitive job market, when opportunities are more limited, the systematic job hunter will inevitably be the luckier one.

Resumes and Cover Letters: How to Make Yours Stand Out

A resume is like the coming attraction for a movie; after seeing it, a prospective employer decides whether or not he wants to see you. If you analyze your audience, your resume will end up on a desk instead of in a wastebasket.

There is nothing difficult or mysterious about writing a resume; nonetheless, plenty of otherwise intelligent people make bungling errors of judgment or carelessness that result in their being knocked out of the job competition in Round 1, before they have really even had a chance to prove themselves.

Here are some simple guidelines for writing your resume based on recommendations from college recruiters and personnel directors.

The Best Format

There are seven major areas to cover in a resume — personal information, job objective, education, job experience, additional information, personal interests, and references, in that order.

Personal information. Put your full name (not nicknames) in the center or the upper right-hand corner of the page (the left-hand corner often gets stapled or clipped to other papers). Follow your name with your home address and phone number at which you can be reached during the day. It is not necessary to include any of the following information on your resume — some of the items mentioned can even work to your disadvantage:

- Date of birth
- Marital status
- Photograph
- Height and weight
- Health
- Religious or political affiliations
- Social Security number

Job objective. Don't make the mistake of using a phrase that sounds as if you have not quite decided what you want to do — "To work in an interesting and challenging job that offers a lot of contact with people." If you're unsure about the exact position you want, at least be specific about the area that interests you. Nothing except the time it takes to type them prevents you from using different job objectives on different resumes, depending on the company and field. Another option: leave your job objective out if you need space, and include it in your cover letter instead.

Education. Unless you have worked in one or more jobs that are directly related to the job you hope to land, this category belongs before Job Experience. Include the names and locations of the colleges and graduate schools from which you earned degrees, and the years they were awarded. Mention your major or curriculum and any academic honors or awards you received. (Include your grade point average only if it's above a 3.0.) If you put yourself through school or paid a major portion of your expenses, be sure to mention that. It shows you are highly motivated and can handle two important demands on your time. If you were a club officer or played a major role in an organization, mention that under a subheading, "Extracurricular Activities." Information about your high school performance is usually not meaningful to a prospective employer.

Job experience. Mention only those part-time or summer jobs or internships that were significant, either because of the length of time you worked or the relevance of the job. List them in chronological order, beginning with the most recent. Include the name, location, and businesses of each company, your dates of employment, and your job title. If you were an intern and the internship was competitive, mention the number of applicants and the number accepted.

Unless a job title is self-explanatory, briefly describe your responsibilities. Quantify them whenever you can — the dollar amount of merchandise you sold, the number of people you taught, or the volume of transactions you put through. If your job was ordinary, be sure to point out any out-of-the-ordinary things you did — taking charge of the office when the boss was on vacation, for instance, or initiating a learn-to-swim program. Don't, however, try to inflate your responsibilities — experienced interviewers are bound to grill you if your qualifications seem overstated.

Additional information. Information that does not fit anywhere else can be included here — skills that are not related to your major, for instance, such as computer programming or fluency in a foreign language. Any certifications (for special courses or seminars you have taken), publications, or presentations can be mentioned here as well.

Personal interests. This is the icebreaker section — interviewers often use the information listed here to start an interview. Mention hobbies, sports, special interests, or travel but include only activities in which you are or were actively involved. There are few things more embarrassing (and damaging) than having an interviewer ask about one of your interests — about which he knows a lot — only to have it turn out to be something you would like to do rather than something you actually have done.

References. You can write "References available on request." It's a good idea to prepare a separate sheet with reference information to give to a prospective employer after an interview.

Additional Pointers

- Keep your resume short. You should be able to fit it all onto one page.
- Make your layout easy to read by leaving lots of white space between categories and underlining and/or capitalizing major items and headings.
- Look up any word you are unsure of. A misspelled word may cost you an interview.
- Type the resume neatly, with no erasures or smudges: be sure that your ribbon is not so worn out that the letters are hard to read. If you are not nimble-fingered, consider having your resume typed professionally or "designed" on a computer. A typeset or laser-jet print job is the most professional looking.
- Have your resume reproduced by offset printing or photocopying.
- Ask a friend whose grammar and spelling are expert to read your resume before you type the final copy. Your school's career planning center also may be willing to critique it.

For more detailed information on resume writing, check out publications in your school's career planning office. Or get a copy of my book *The 90-Minute Resume.*

Offbeat Resumes

Traditional employers in banking, insurance, accounting, or law probably will write you off as an oddball if you send anything but a traditional resume. But recruiters and personnel directors say that a smartly packaged resume that reflects your originality can be a real asset if you are applying for a job in a creative field.

The most common reason students send an unusual resume is to stand out from the hordes of their peers with similar credentials who are applying for the same job. Cheryl Steinberg wanted a job as a copywriter at an advertising agency. She entitled her resume "Where Have I Been All Your Life?" and went on to describe her background, experience, and objectives in short, humorous paragraphs. Her unique approach worked: 98 percent of the employers to whom she sent it contacted her, and many of them invited her to come in for an interview.

Another legitimate reason for sending a nontraditional resume is to feature aspects of your experience that don't fit into a standard format. Rhonda Gainer, an apparel-design major, wanted to include short descriptions of several independent projects. She folded an 8½-by-11-inch sheet into a brochure and had the text typeset into three columns.

Cover Letters

Sending a resume without a cover letter is like ordering a pizza without any extras; it's acceptable, but hardly mouth-watering. To achieve its purpose, a cover letter should be short, to the point, and tailor-made for each prospective employer. Its purpose is to tell a firm why you're the person it's looking for. An ideal cover letter runs three paragraphs. Introduce yourself in the first: mention the position that interests you, how you heard about it, and who suggested you write. In paragraph two, explain why you are interested in and qualified for the position, company, or field. Don't quote from your resume; give more details about a particular achievement or job that should impress this particular employer. In the last paragraph, request an interview. The fastest way to get a response is to say that you will call in a week. Waiting to hear from an employer can take weeks, depending on his backload or hiring situation.

If you can communicate your enthusiasm in your letter, you are more likely to get invited in for an interview. That can take a lot of thought. If a company is an underdog, for example, you might mention that you would like to be a part of a team that will take on "the big guys." If it's a well-established firm, you might mention how you became interested in the company — a friend who worked there and liked it, a professor who talked about it in class — and the qualities of the firm that particularly attract you.

On-Campus Recruitment: Are Assembly-Line Interviews Worthwhile?

During the spring term — and sometimes the fall — college placement offices take on the appearance of giant personnel factories. In closet-size cubicles with thin walls, interviewers in the uniform of their company meet face-to-face with nervous students, most of whom are made even more uncomfortable by ties and heels and suits, which have replaced down vests, jeans, and tennis shoes.

On-campus recruitment is often *the* most effective way for M.B.A. and law school students to find jobs. That's because the placement offices of these schools put great importance on finding jobs for their grads, and both employers and students have a much better idea of each other's qualifications and what they want.

Not surprisingly, the undergraduate students most likely to find jobs through on-campus recruiting are those majoring in business, engineering, computer science, and other technical fields. But you shouldn't pass up this "backyard" job-finding strategy if you aren't in a highly marketable major or at the top of your class. It is a good way to sharpen your interviewing skills and get an even better idea of the kind of job you are looking for.

The on-campus recruitment works this way. Employers — generally large companies who can project their employment needs months in advance and who have the money to send recruiters to colleges — contact your school's placement office about scheduling a one- to three-day visit to the campus during the recruiting season. At many schools, recruiting takes place in the fall — October or November — or winter — January or February. At Michigan State University, which has one of the biggest recruiting schedules in the country (about 3,500 employers visit the campus annually), recruiting is done October through May.

You can often find out which employers plan to visit your campus in the fall as early as June. But recruitment lineups are not usually formally announced until the month before interviews begin. Some placement offices send out a schedule to all seniors; at other schools, you may have to go to the placement office to find out when recruiters are coming.

Most interviewers will specify the kinds of applicants they want to see by listing the majors that would best qualify for job openings they anticipate. Between 20 and 38 percent prescreen applicants because they can only see a limited number of students and prefer to see the ones they feel are the most promising candidates. Most companies decide whom to interview by reviewing resumes — another good reason for making sure that yours is top-notch. Some also request a credential file, which usually contains a transcript and letters of recommendation from previous employers. The courses you took are usually a major factor in their decision to interview you. Regardless of what interview sign-up method is used at your school, it pays to keep checking back with your placement office since "late" recruiters often contact the school after the majority have already put in their requests.

Before you decide to sign up for an interview with a particular company, you should check out all the information your placement office has on it (most companies usually provide annual reports, descriptive brochures, and job description material) and talk to your placement director about the kinds of students who have received job offers from that employer in the past.

On some campuses, it is relatively easy to sign up for interviews; all you need do is go to the placement office and put your name on a list to see a particular employer. If an "in-demand" employer does not prescreen applications, interviews are set up on a first-come, first-served basis. At some schools, that may mean resorting to a popular concert-ticket tactic — camping out at the door of the placement office in order to assure yourself a place in line.

An increasing number of schools are using computerized lists to avoid that problem. Students fill out a registration form and sometimes a "form" resume (they are easier for employers to read through quickly) and are then sent a request form. You indicate which companies interest you in order of preference (there is usually a maximum of ten to fifteen you can list) and the times when you are available for interviews. Provided your qualifications suit the employer's needs, the faster you return your card, the better your chances for getting an interview. (It pays, of course, to be flexible with interview times.) Once an interviewer's slots are filled, you are put on a waiting list; if there are enough students on it, the company may decide to send an additional recruiter; if not, you are the alternate should a student on the "confirmed" list decide to cancel.

If you are unsuccessful in your initial attempts to get an interview with one of your top-priority companies (because you either did not get there first or did not make it through the prescreening), you may be able to wangle an interview in one of several ways. First, try talking to the placement director — if you can show why you are particularly qualified for a job at that company, he may "fit" you into the schedule. Another alternative is to show up a half hour before the first appointment is scheduled; many interviewers will appreciate your motivation and talk to you then. If that is not possible, ask if there is any other time during their stay when the two of you might get together. If the interviewer is up to his neck in scheduled interviews your best bet is to try to schedule an appointment with the college recruitment office at the company's headquarters.

It is a good idea to regularly visit your school's placement office, whether or not it is recruiting season, to check new listings on its job bulletin board. Get to know your placement director; if he is aware of your interests, he is more likely to think of you should he get a call from a prospective employer who is looking for someone with your qualifications.

The Self-Initiated Search: Stalking the Elusive Job Opening

Why aren't some of the most desirable entry-level jobs advertised or posted on job-placement-office bulletin boards? Because they are snatched up by job hunters who have put out feelers through a network of people they know or have met in their job campaign.

The best way to hook into the hidden job market is to contact employers directly. This approach is the most time-consuming, but it also is one of the best ways to land the job you want.

Locating Prospective Employers

Begin by getting a copy of the *College Placement Annual* from your college placement office (some give it out for free; others charge a small fee). The book contains a comprehensive listing of employers, the types of openings they have for college graduates, and whom to contact about a job.

There are several other good directories, but none of them give information on specific types of job openings for college graduates. They can, however, give you a more complete picture of companies and organizations in your field. Most of those listed below are available in the reference section of your school's general or business library.

- *Million Dollar Directory* (Dun's Marketing Services) provides general information on approximately 115,000 businesses in the United States, including headquarters address and phone number, annual sales, number of employees, division names, and function or lines of business and more.

- *Standard and Poor's Register of Corporations, Directors and Executives* provides information about 45,000 corporations and their top executives.

- *Business Organizations and Agencies Directory* (Gale Research Company) lists a wide variety of organizations, agencies, and services in business and industry. Major categories include chambers of commerce, franchise companies, hotel-motel systems, and databanks and computerized services and many others.

- *Contacts Influential* provides data about small companies or local offices of large companies by specific metropolitan areas. Each entry provides the firm name and address, key personnel by name and title, the age of the business, and the number of employees as well as other information.

- *Business Newsbank* (NewsBank, Inc.) is a reference service providing the full text of business articles selected from newspaper and business journals in over 400 U.S. cities. Stories feature new and emerging companies, developments in large companies, business people moving up and out, and new products and technologies.

There are numerous smaller directories that are aimed at specific fields, among them *Polk's World Bank Directory, Standard Directory of Advertising Agencies,* and *Mental Health Directory.* Check *Bibliography of Directories, Handbooks, and Guides* to find ones in your field.

In addition to these sources, ask your placement director for his suggestions on local employers. The yellow pages is probably the best geographic reference book, especially for small businesses and organizations.

You will probably have to contact at least twenty-five employers to get several interviews — more than that if you are in a highly competitive field.

Developing Company Profiles

Most job seekers skip this step because they are eager to set up interviews. But the more you know about a company, the better an idea you'll have of where you would fit in best. That's preferable to letting the personnel department, which often is not aware of all the needs of the company, make that decision for you.

If the companies on your list are large corporations or leaders in their field, there probably are articles about them in the business or general media. The five best indexes are:

- *Business Periodicals Index*
- *Wall Street Journal Index*
- *New York Times Index*
- *Where to Find Business Information,* by David M. Brownstone and Gordon Carruth
- *Everybody's Business, An Almanac: The Irreverent Guide to Corporate America,* edited by Milton Moskowitz, Michael Katz, and Robert Levery.

Track down the articles and read them (your school's business library probably has the most material). You may find a gold mine of inside facts and figures, or you may have to search the story for nuggets of information.

If the businesses you are considering are small ones, check with the local newspaper for stories that have appeared in the last year. Another good source of articles is trade publications.

What kind of information can be helpful to you as a job hunter?

- Expanding areas of the company or industry
- High turnover areas
- A company merger or takeover (that often creates new job opportunities)
- A company's major competitors
- A company's most successful and least successful products
- Problems the company or industry is facing
- Projected personnel needs in specific areas
- Legislation or political issues that affect the industry

Some of this information can help you judge which department or companies to contact; the usefulness of other facts may not be evident until you are actually interviewing with that company and can ask good questions or make insightful comments based on your knowledge.

Making Contact

You're ready to talk to a select group of employers, but now you have to persuade them to see you. There are two ways to set up an interview.

The first, contacting the personnel department or manager, has several drawbacks:

1. The job of the personnel department is to screen applicants, not hire them, so getting an appointment is the first in a series of hurdles you will have to jump before you get to the person with hiring power.

2. Some personnel departments are ineffective — they may not know how to do their job well, or their hands may be tied by the politics of the organization.

3. The personnel department may be reluctant to see you — or even refuse to — if you are not calling in response to a specific job opening; you are just another hour's work in an overcrowded day.

Check out the reputation of a personnel department by asking an alumnus, friend, or relative who works for the company, or your placement director.

Even if the personnel department is well run, a better approach is to write directly to the department head or executive for whom you would like to work. If he is looking for someone with your credentials, he probably will interview you himself — or recommend you to someone else in the company. If he's not, he may still see you.

"Interviewing for information" (asking employers for advice rather than an interview) is a widely used strategy for looking for a job without looking as if you are. Employers, of course, know that too, but if you are sincere about a request for advice, most people will talk to you. It is usually easier to get in to see the person who is just below a department head. He usually has more time and fewer such requests, and he can recommend you to his boss if he is impressed. Don't ask personnel directors for this kind of advice unless you are going into the personnel field.

In your letter or phone call, be sure to explain who you are, why you have contacted this person, and what you want to talk to him about.

If you make a good impression on the person you talk to, he may:

- Get in touch with you if he hears of an appropriate job opening.
- Recommend you to someone else in the company who has hiring power.
- Give you the names, if you ask, of other people you might contact.

What is the fastest way to get through to someone for an interview or advice? That depends on your style. Here are the limitations and advantages of three alternatives:

1. *The telephone call.* This usually is the quickest way to find out if a person will see you and when, and it works well for people who have engaging phone personalities. But be prepared to deal with secretaries who protect their bosses from "unsolicited" phone calls the way bodyguards protect rock stars from backstage fans. You may have to make several calls if you don't have a person's name. If the secretary sounds friendly, ask her advice. She may make a special effort to sandwich you in between appointments if you get her on your side.

If she does not ask why you are calling but tells you that her boss is unavailable, don't leave your number and ask him to return the call. He probably won't. Instead, ask the secretary if she would suggest a good time for you to call back. If you still can't get through after several attempts, try calling before 9 or after 5, when the person you're trying to reach is likely to answer his own phone.

2. *The letter.* Two problems about letters are (1) they take several days to arrive (and sometimes never make it at all) and (2) they often get misplaced if they do make it to their address. But if you feel you come across better on paper, write to the person you want to see — and follow up with a phone call. A letter is also a good fallback if you have been unsuccessful in repeated attempts to get through by phone.

Always address a letter to a specific person, not merely to a title or "To whom it may concern." If you do not know who the appropriate person is, find out. (If the switchboard operator cannot help you, have her put you through to the right department.) Make sure that you get the correct spelling and the person's title — a mistake may end up costing you an interview.

3. *The drop-in.* This tack works best if you are simply trying to get an appointment with someone in the personnel department or if you are applying to a small firm. It's harder for most people to say no to a body than to a voice — even if it is impossible to see you at that very moment.

Contacts: The Who-You-Know Strategy Works

Kate White heard about an opening for a political organizer through the public relations director at her college, who knew Kate was interested in working in a campaign. Kate followed up on the lead and landed the job.

Rather than making a cold call to a company, Rhonda Gainer asked a contact she had made during a summer internship if she knew anyone there. She did. Rhonda called him and made such a good impression that he created a new position for her.

Androc Kislevitz's first job was manning the complaint line at a local newspaper. Six weeks into the job, he got a gripe call from someone who, he discovered during their conversation, knew his parents. Andy confided that he hated the job and was on the lookout for a more promising publishing position. The caller put Andy in touch with a big book publishing honcho, who hired him as his assistant.

All three people relied on the most valuable foot-in-the-door technique a job-hunter can use: the contact connection. More than half of all working professionals land new jobs through contacts. Although the percentage of people who land their first job that way is much lower, the contact connection is the way to beat the odds, because usually only a few people are competing for a particular job.

Who is a contact? Anyone who has the power to hire you, introduce you to someone who can hire you, or give you information about a job opening. (Unless the contact is your father and he is the president of the company, you will, of course, still have to sell yourself.) You can get suggestions for contacts from professors, former employees, friends of your parents, relatives, or neighbors.

While it is true that the who-you-know strategy works best if your family is well connected in the community or in your field, your most useful contacts may be people you have met on your own, among them alumni and professionals you interview for information.

If you are moving to a new area, consider working for a temporary employment agency that specializes in your field. That's a good way to make contacts at different companies (and "sample" an organization before you apply for a job).

The one thing you should be wary of if you use this job-hunting strategy is misusing a contact's name. If a contact tells you about a job or gives you the name of someone to speak to, be sure to ask your contact if you can use his name and whether he would recommend your doing so. (He may not be on good terms with the person who is doing the hiring.)

Your contact may offer to call ahead for you to let his friend know you will be getting in touch. If you contact the person yourself, explain who you are, that your contact suggested you call, and what kind of job (or advice) you are looking for. Ask when it would be convenient for him to talk with you — you have to be flexible when you are asking someone for a favor.

Even if your contact isn't in a position to hire you, he will probably want to meet you before recommending you to someone else. If there are no job openings at that company, ask your contact if there are other people he suggests you call. The whole point of contacts is to keep making more of them — until you land the job you want.

Job Fairs: The Smorgasbord Approach to Meeting Employers

You can talk to dozens of employers in one day at a job fair, which is usually held in a large auditorium filled with booths where you can meet representatives of participating companies. Job fairs are often geared to recruiting people with skills in fields such as data processing, engineering, or nursing. But an increasing number are open to job hunters in a wide variety of fields, particularly those looking for entry-level jobs. Job fairs are often sponsored by chambers of commerce, a consortium of colleges, and newspapers.

You can maximize the use of your time by following these steps.

1. *Get an advance list of the companies who will be participating.* They are sometimes listed in advertisements in your local newspaper that appear prior to the job fair. That way, you can identify the companies you most want to visit in advance.

2. *Bring up-to-date copies of your resume.* And dress as if you were going on a job interview.

3. *Make your visit with each employer on your list.* First ask whether the company offers the kind of job or jobs you are interested in. Then briefly describe your skills. If you are willing to relocate, say so — the company may be able to place you out of the area if no openings exist locally.

4. *Collect the cards of the employers you meet.* Follow up with a short letter to those you would like to work for.

5. *Don't expect an on-the-spot job offer.* While the people you talk to at a job fair may have the power to hire you, they generally invite you to come to their offices for further interviews before an offer is made.

In addition to finding out about specific openings, you can pick up other useful information at job fairs, including:

- The academic credentials employers want for certain jobs
- Unpublicized internship or cooperative education programs
- Whom to contact about a job opening in another area if the division of the company represented at the fair only hires certain majors

Your placement office or the local chamber of commerce can tell you about upcoming fairs. They are often advertised in local newspapers, too.

Employment Agencies: Are They Looking Out for You or Trying to Make a Fast Buck?

> Exciting, diversified entry-level spot available. Excellent opportunity to learn biz from inside and become truly involved. Ability to work well with people and eagerness to learn a must. Truly a growth situation for the right individual. Contact Pie-in-the-Sky Unlimited Employment Agency immed.

It sounds too good to be true, but it's tempting enough for you to pay a visit.

That's the purpose of teaser ads, which frequently are either too general or are descriptions of jobs that don't exist. Most reputable employment agencies advertise their best "real" job openings, although they may sound less inviting when you find out the details.

A frequent complaint about employment agencies — that the personnel are not personable — will have no serious impact on your job campaign (although it can bruise fragile job-seeking egos). But another complaint — being sent to interviews for jobs that don't interest you — can have major ramifications. When Michael Simon graduated from college with a major in political science, he had no clear idea of the job he wanted. The employment agency he visited offered him the selling jobs typically offered to male graduates. He took a job as a management trainee for an industrial service company. His second job — a sales-trainee position — also came via an employment agency. After three years on two jobs he didn't much enjoy, Michael became a stockbroker with a major national firm — a job he got on his own.

Some college graduates *do* find good entry-level jobs in a career field they stick with through employment agencies. Leslie Thompson Williams got started in media sales through an employment-agency placement. The job was a secretarial position, but she moved up to a job as sales coordinator within six months.

If you decide to use an employment agency as one part of your job search, heed the advice of people who have gone that route:

- Steer clear of agencies where you pay the job-finding fee. At reputable agencies, employers foot the bill.

- Do not agree to an exclusive listing with the agency — that means you will not patronize its competitors. It only limits your options.

- Avoid getting lassoed into "extras" the agency offers — resume or interview workshops, for instance, or vocational tests. Agencies often charge high fees for services you can get free, as an alumnus, at your school's placement office. In the case of vocational testing, agencies may not be qualified to interpret your results.

- Before you patronize an agency, check to see whether it is listed in *The Membership Directory by Specialization of the National Association of Personnel Consultants*. The 2,300 members listed subscribe to a code of ethics developed by the association. The directory can be found in many university and large public libraries.

- Use an agency that specializes in your field. About two thirds of the agencies who belong to the National Association of Personnel Consultants cater to job hunters in particular fields such as data processing, financial services, and publishing. Agencies list their specialties in advertisements in the yellow pages or in the help-wanted section of Sunday newspapers.

State Employment Agencies

State employment services, also called employment security offices, charge neither the employee nor the employer a fee. Some government agencies and all federal contractors are required to list job openings with them, although the majority of the openings are for nonprofessional positions. You can find the nearest state employment agency by looking in the white pages under your state's Department of Labor, Job Service Division.

Help-Wanted Ads: Stacked Deck?

Judging by the help-wanted ads in any major metropolitan newspaper, you might get the impression that jobs are there for the asking. That's usually true only for students in highly marketable majors.

Just how bad are the odds? Ads for glamour jobs may pull hundreds of inquiries. Even run-of-the-mill positions elicit dozens. Most replies to help-wanted ads end up in the wastebasket; only well-known companies that identify themselves in an ad bother to send you even a "thanks, but no thanks" letter of acknowledgment.

But if you're a gambler or if you're a conscientious job hunter who covers all his bases, you will lose nothing but time by responding to help-wanted ads.

If you are just beginning your job search, the classifieds can give you good ballpark information on:

- Salary ranges for jobs in your field
- Job requirements
- The abundance (or dearth) of job openings in your field

You can raise the odds of at least getting a response by screening the ads. Those that mention a specific job title and nitty-gritty responsibilities indicate at least one thing: that the job probably exists. Ads that mention the employer's name, or, better yet, the name of the person to contact, are better than blind ads that give only a post-office box number.

Check sections of the newspaper that your competition may not notice. The classifieds in the business section, for example, are sprinkled with ads for advertising promotion writers, occupational therapists, and academic counselors. Investigate professional and trade journals, too. Fewer people see these ads, although those who do may have better credentials.

Another tactic is to scan ads for high-level positions in your field (particularly if the ad mentions heading a new department). Write to the employer, explain you are interested in an entry-level position in the new department, and ask for an interview. There may not be a job for a while, but, since it won't have been advertised, the odds will be more in your favor.

If you decide to respond to a help-wanted ad, keep the following in mind:

- Always send a cover letter with your resume. If no specific name or title of the person to contact is given, avoid offending anyone. Address it to "Personnel Director" or "Department Manager."
- Write a different cover letter to each employer and highlight those skills and experiences that seem to meet the qualifications mentioned in the ad.

- If salary requirements are requested, it is probably best to give a range and add that you are flexible.

Government Jobs: How to Apply to the Country's Biggest Employer

Uncle Sam hires about 15,000 graduates with science and engineering degrees and between 5,000 and 8,000 liberal arts and business graduates for administrative positions annually. Most of the positions are trainee slots for professional jobs, and starting salaries are competitive.

Most college graduates are hired at the GS-5 or GS-7 level, which in early 1991 paid salaries of $17,805 and $22,052, respectively. Those who are assigned to federal jobs in New York, Los Angeles, and San Francisco earn an additional 8 percent (to compensate for the higher cost of living in those areas). Engineers and scientists in scarce skill areas often start at the top of their grade and earn even more. With a master's degree, you can start at GS-9 at almost $27,000.

Those with engineering and science backgrounds are referred directly to agencies for interviews. Graduates who have majored in liberal arts, the social sciences, business, or other areas must take the Administrative Careers with America Test (which is given at least two times a year) unless their grade point average is 3.5 or higher. The high GPA means you can be hired directly by an agency.

There are six exams within the Administrative Careers with America Test, each of which corresponds to a job family. They are:

Group 1 — Health, safety, and the environment

Group 2 — Writing and public information

Group 3 — Business, finance, and management

Group 4 — Personnel, administration, and computers

Group 5 — Benefits review, tax, and legal

Group 6 — Law enforcement and investigation

You can take one exam — or all six. How high you score affects how quickly you will be considered by the agencies that have positions open in your area. If you score 90, for example, you will be tapped sooner than the person who scores 80. You can avoid the ranking process only if you are bilingual or have a bicultural background. If, for example, you speak Spanish and an opening in a federal agency in the Southwest requires that language capability, you could be hired over someone who scored higher on the test but who did not speak Spanish.

If you think you may be interested in a position with the federal government, start by checking out the *Federal Career Directory*, which is available in your college planning and placement office. It describes the federal agencies and the kinds of positions each offers. Or you can call the College Hotline (1-900-990-9200). You will be asked (by a voice messaging system) questions about your academic record and job interests and given information about how to apply for an entry-level position. If you leave your name and address, you will be sent an application. Callers usually spend 3 to 4 minutes on the phone at a cost of 40 cents a minute; still, it's faster and usually cheaper than going to a Federal Job Information Center.

Some federal agencies do on-campus recruiting, particularly to fill engineering and scientific positions. If you have already graduated, you can find out about current openings through *Federal Career Opportunities*, a biweekly publication put out by Federal Research Service, Inc., P.O. Box 1059, Vienna, VA 22183-1059. It also publishes the book *How to Get a Federal Job* and a series entitled "Federal Job Winner's Tips."

5

The Interview

Preparation: Curing the Interview Jitters . . .
Applications and Tests: What You Should Know
About Them . . . First Impressions: How to Make
Them Work for You . . . Q and A: What You
Will Be Grilled on and What to Ask . . . Eating
Out: What to Do If the Interview Includes a
Meal . . . A Bad Interview: How to Get It Back
on the Right Track . . . Follow-Up: It Can Make
All the Difference . . . Rejection: How to Cope
with It . . . Evaluating a Job Offer: What to
Consider Before You Accept

This is it. The final exam to end all final exams. Granted, there is no blue
book, and you will not get a letter grade. But how well you "test" may
play a major role in determining your fate, possibly for the next few
years. Understandably, you're nervous. The butterflies are dive-bombing against your stomach lining, and your antiperspirant is out to lunch.

Relax. This may be your first interview, but it certainly is not going to
be your last. You may as well learn to be a good player at this game,
because the stakes are high. Take heart; as with most skills, interviewing
improves with practice.

Dwelling on the real purpose of the interview probably will only
increase your anxiety, but it is worth repeating. If you understand how
subjective the process is, you can don the armor necessary to keep your
self-image intact. The main thing the interviewer is trying to determine is
whether he likes you. Of course, he's concerned with your interest in the
company and your qualifications: the interview will come to a crashing
halt if the company is looking for a junior volcanologist and you have
never taken physics or geology. The woods are full of people similarly
interested and qualified. But if the interviewer concludes that you're a
normal, pleasant, likable human being (if you remind him of himself or

of people he likes, that's even better), he may recommend you for the job — or hire you himself.

Unless you are applying to a small company that has no personnel department, expect at least two and possibly as many as eight interviews before you are actually offered a job.

There are several different kinds of interviews; the scenario changes depending on whether you're in a screening interview (a preliminary conversation), a checkout interview (usually your second or "callback" interview), or a hiring interview (the make-or-break session).

The interviewing hierarchy often is set up so that you will deal with the following people in each type of job interview:

- *Screening interview.* An interviewer from the personnel, college re-cruitment, manpower training, or human resources department (the last three are fancy names for personnel departments with additional or specialized functions) *or* a staff member (his usual job is something other than interviewing).

- *Checkout interview.* A higher-up in one of the personnel depart-ments mentioned above, more staff people, the head honcho of the department or company.

- *Hiring interview.* The person who will be your boss, his boss.

Here is the lowdown on interviewing — from what to ask to what to wear to how to cope with rejection. Remember, be yourself. You have no doubt heard that before, but the simplicity and truthfulness of this adage can pay off if you take it to heart.

Preparation: Curing the Interview Jitters

The most frequent mistakes job applicants make are:

- Not knowing what kind of job they want

- Being unable to articulate their expectations

- Being unsure of why they are applying to that company

If you are guilty of the first problem, get your act together before you start interviewing. If you are afflicted with the second, practice answer-ing questions about your goals before you set foot in any interviewer's office. Problem three can be avoided if you use the research techniques described in the "Self-Initiated Search" in Chapter 4, "The Job Cam-paign." While it is always an advantage to know as much as you can about a company, it's probably more important in a screening interview to be familiar with the industry. If you are asked to come in for a second interview, make sure you find out information about the company itself.

Use the Q and A section of this chapter to help you think about how you will answer the questions interviewers love to ask and what ques-tions you will ask them.

In the sense that a screening interview will determine whether you get any further with an employer, it's the most difficult interview of all. You can make the most of it if you:

- *Diffuse the sweaty-palms syndrome by going through a mock interview with a friend, parent, professor, or placement office counselor.* Many placement offices conduct interview workshops; some even have videotape facilities so that you can critique your performance.
- *Read the newspaper before your interview.* Many interviewers start the interview with small talk or evaluate how well you can think on your feet by asking your opinion of a late-breaking news event. You don't want to be in the embarrassing position of not having heard about it.

Applications and Tests: What You Should Know About Them

Job Applications — A Few Precautions

Unless you are applying for a job as a cowboy, clam shucker, or artichoke picker, there is virtually no way to escape filling out a job application if you want to get an interview.

After you have filled out your tenth application, you may begin to lose sight of the importance placed on this document by the people in personnel. Whatever number application it is, keep the following things in mind:

1. Make sure you put down a telephone number at which you can be reached. If the employer cannot get hold of you, he may decide to move down the list to your competition.

2. If you are a recently married woman using your husband's last name, include your maiden name on the application so that your references and records can be checked without confusion.

3. Do not write "See resume" under "Job Experience." That indicates laziness, a quality employers loathe.

4. If you are asked to state your salary expectations, put "Negotiable" or a salary range. Keep it within hailing distance of the going rate for an entry-level person in your field. If you put down what you would like to get paid, you may be written off immediately as too high-priced.

5. If you are physically disabled and the application asks whether you have any physical limitations or special health conditions, you can do one of two things: leave the space blank and deal with the situation in the interview (although the employer may be put off by the surprise), or be honest about your condition, explaining briefly how it would not interfere with your ability to do the job. Do not be afraid to bring up the subject of the type of accommodation you will need on the job and what its cost will probably be, if any (it could be as simple as rearranging furniture).

6. If the application does not ask for information you think might help the interviewer better evaluate you, be sure to include it.

Preemployment Tests—Are You Capable, Highly Motivated, Honest, and Drug-Free?

Interviews are subjective, and reference checks do not always uncover potential problems because many employers are reluctant to give out information beyond a former employee's job title and dates of employment for fear of a lawsuit. So many employers are adding tests to their selection process.

The controversy over whether these tests are valid, fair to the applicant, or in violation of his privacy is being argued in many courts and legislatures. The bottom line, however, is this: if you want to be considered for a job, you must agree to take the tests that the employer routinely administers to job candidates applying for that position.

Here are some of the most widely administered tests, what they measure, and how employers use them in the selection process.

Aptitude tests. Aside from drug tests, these make up the most widely used type of prescreening tests by employers of recent graduates; some 25 percent of all employers say they use them.

Probably the most common is the typing test. Even though the job title may not contain the word "typist," your ability to use a keyboard may be a factor in landing the job. That's certainly true in many entry-level communications jobs, which involve creating and producing the written word on a typewriter or computer. Find out in advance if typing is likely to be a requirement; if it is, practice before you go to the interview. You may not be ushered in for an interview if your typing isn't up to snuff.

Beyond typing tests, the most common types of competence tests are likely to be given in specific skill areas such as computer programming and accounting. You may not be able to prepare in advance, since most are designed to measure your knowledge of a subject area. But it pays to ask whether a competence test will be given so that you can prepare yourself mentally.

Personality tests. About 15 percent of employers use personality tests in the prescreening process. Their purpose: to test workplace-type traits and mental attitudes necessary to succeed in a particular job, business, or organization. Personality tests are often given to managers, professionals, and salespeople.

One such test is the Profile Work Behavior Test, which asks job applicants to respond to self-descriptive items about their energy level, tendency to follow rules, policies and procedures, organization of work habits, motivation to do a good job, friendliness level, assertiveness, stick-to-itiveness, preference to work alone or with others, level of emotional maturity, and frequency of arguing. The cognitive abilities it measures are your speed of solving work problems, interest in a business career, memory for details, vocabulary, ability to quickly and accurately notice small details, and mechanical interest.

Those in favor of personality tests say that the subjective judgment of an interviewer creates more possibility for discrimination. Opponents question the validity of the tests and their added potential for pigeonholing people into the wrong slot.

Integrity tests. Prior to 1988, most employers who were concerned about employee theft used the polygraph, or lie detector, test to screen out undesirable employees. Then Congress banned most private employers from using it because it did not consistently yield valid results; in other words, honest people could fail the test and lose out on an employment opportunity.

Between 5,000 and 6,000 employers now use honesty and integrity tests in the screening process. Job hunters who are looking for jobs as convenience store employees or retail clerks are asked to take these tests more often than those seeking other positions.

Most integrity tests are pen-and-pencil tests and are designed to measure whether a person is likely to commit on-the-job theft (stealing money and/or property) or engage in counterproductive behavior (lateness, abuse of sick leave, participation in strikes, and absenteeism).

Questions may be direct: "How prompt are you?" "Do you think it is stealing to take small items home from work?" "Have you ever been disgusted with yourself because you did something dishonest?" Or they may be veiled-purpose questions: "Do you make your bed?" "How often are you embarrassed?" "Would you ever talk back to a boss or a teacher?"

Test manufacturers and employers who use them believe that the tests are a valid and effective way to spot problem workers before they are hired. Psychologists, members of Congress, and civil libertarians are concerned, however, about their potential for misuse.

A report commissioned by Congress found that existing research did not clearly confirm or refute that integrity tests can accurately predict dishonest behavior in the workplace. It found that integrity tests are essentially personality tests, which are designed to identify individual traits and behaviors. The unanswered questions are whether or not honesty is a psychological trait and, if it is, how it should be defined in the workplace.

Drug testing. Some 20 million jobs are held by workers who use illegal drugs such as marijuana, amphetamines, cocaine, and crack. And experts claim that drug and alcohol abuse is costing employers $100-billion a year through losses in productivity, accidents, absenteeism, and medical expenses.

It's no surprise then that between 40 and 50 percent of private employers ask candidates to agree to take a drug test. And 20 to 30 percent more plan to add that step to their selection and hiring process. The Drug-Free Workplace Act, which went into effect in 1989, mandates that corporations doing business with the federal government conduct drug tests as part of the hiring process. (Only a quarter of employers test for alcohol use, even though it remains the most serious substance-abuse problem.)

The most common type of drug test is the relatively inexpensive urinalysis, which measures traces of drugs. Cocaine can be detected as long as three days after consumption, while marijuana may be evident up to three weeks after use. One of the problems with urine tests is that they sometimes give false positives — over-the-counter aspirin, for example, can show up as an illegal drug on some tests.

So far, most courts have upheld the legality of preemployment drug testing.

First Impressions: How to Make Them Work for You

Whether you're asked back for a second interview may be determined during the first 5 minutes of your screening interview. Seem incredible? Just think back to a blind date and how immediately you formed your impression during your first few minutes of conversation. Despite the deluge of advice on the subject, there is no magic formula for coming across positively to every interviewer you meet. But if you keep the suggestions offered in this section in mind, you should at least be able to avoid turning anyone off.

How You Look

John "Dress for Success" Molloy would have had a field day with the outfits I wore on my first job interviews. Granted, it was the early seventies when a more casual look was acceptable, but I can understand now why one personnel agency counselor suggested I go shopping before I went for interviews. Picture this: For the screening interview — a full-length purple polyester dress, slit up to the knee. Long bell-shaped sleeves in a contrasting lavender color. The crowning touch — a crooked star (I was no talented seamstress), also in lavender, appliquéd on the bodice. For the callback interview — black sailor pants, puckered white T-shirt, and Indian beads. Fortunately, a certain degree of eccentricity was tolerated at the magazine that hired me.

Your appearance, quite simply, should not interfere with your being considered for a job. But be forewarned — inappropriate attire causes many interviewers to write off candidates they might otherwise hire. Most employers prefer the classic to the trendy, the modest to the sexy, and the low-key to the distracting in both clothes and hairstyle.

The best rule of thumb on dressing for an interview is: your clothes should match the job for which you are applying — that is, the outfit should be one you would wear on an important day if you got the job.

Suits are not appropriate for every kind of interview — an open-necked shirt or turtleneck worn with a sports jacket would fit the bill in a graphic arts department. A simple dress would be fine for a health-field position for which employees wear uniforms.

If you buy new clothes for job interviews, be sure to give them a test run. It's better not to find out during an interview that your collar is too tight. It is not necessary to drain your bank account—employers don't expect recent grads to wear expensive clothes.

If getting a job with a particular company is very important to you, try to find out what their upwardly mobile employees wear. (How their recruiter dresses is a good clue.) It is human nature to be more favorably inclined toward someone who looks the part.

Here is a checklist of it-goes-without-saying reminders about appearance, which I might not have included if it weren't for my own slipups: I once sat sweaty palmed reading a newspaper while waiting to be seen. After we shook hands, the interviewer mentioned pleasantly that it looked as if I had been shoveling coal.

Appearance "Musts"

- Clean, manicured nails
- Neat hair
- Polished shoes
- Natural-looking makeup
- Long-sleeved shirts if wearing a suit

To Be Avoided

- Baggy stockings or saggy socks
- Perfumes or colognes
- Tassels or shiny buckles on shoes
- Costume jewelry
- Bow ties
- Hair jewelry (if it's functional, it's okay)
- For men, gold chains (unless you are applying for a job as a social director at Club Med) or earrings
- Boots

If you plan to arrive a few minutes early, you will have time to do a rest-room check to make sure that nothing is askew.

Leave any extra baggage—rubbers, umbrella, overcoat, packages—in the waiting room. Unless you have something to show or give the interviewer (other than a resume), leave the portfolio or briefcase at home.

How to Talk

A few, quick pointers:

- When you first meet the interviewer, say, "It is nice to meet you, Mr. _____." (If you're unsure of the interviewer's name, ask the receptionist for it when you arrive.) Dropping his name into the conversation once or twice is a nice touch.
- Speak up; mumblers don't make it.

- Avoid saying, "Have a nice day," when you leave; it's pedestrian and some people loathe it.

Body Language

Saying the right thing with your nonverbal communication is a matter of a few commonsense guidelines:

1. *A good handshake.* If your grip is not firm and confident, practice. If you have a sweaty-palms problem, use a handkerchief immediately before the big moment.

2. *A friendly smile and laugh.* Act as if you are looking forward to the interview. Don't hesitate to inject a little humor into the conversation if it comes easily—and the interviewer isn't acting as if he just came from a funeral. But don't get carried away; a constant smile will only make your jaw muscles ache, and your interviewer will wonder if you had more than Wheaties for breakfast. If you punctuate your sentences with giggles, the interviewer may question your mental stability.

3. *Acceptable posture.* Slumping or slouching is taboo, and avoid crossing and uncrossing your legs too often. Face the interviewer squarely, even if that means repositioning your chair. If you have a choice, choose a chair that puts you at eye level with your interviewer and forces you to sit upright rather than lounge back.

4. *Good nose contact.* True, most interview manuals stress eye contact; if you can't manage that, focusing on the bridge of a person's nose will give him the sensation that you're looking him in the eye. But shift your gaze from time to time—staring is almost as bad as looking out the window.

5. *No smoking.* Unless it is a second or third interview, the atmosphere is relaxed, and the interviewer lights up and offers you a cigarette, smoking can be hazardous to success.

Q and A: What You Will Be Grilled on and What to Ask

Many first-job hunters figure the interviewer will call the shots during the interview, that he has specific questions, and that their role is to answer them. In fact, most interviews are more give-and-take than that.

How skillful an interviewer is depends on his experience; the only people you can assume have a lot of that are personnel interviewers. Campus recruiters are sometimes not savvy interviewers. That means you have to be prepared for the best (sharp, probing questions) and the worst (irrelevant questions or no questions at all). You'll be prepared if you follow these rules:

1. Listen to what the interviewer is saying (even if it's not very interesting). If you let your mind wander, you will bungle your response if the interviewer pops in a quick question.

2. If you don't understand a question, say so or rephrase the question in your own words to make sure that is what he meant.

3. Do not try to outpsych the interviewer by saying things you think he wants to hear — skilled interviewers often rephrase questions to see if your answers are consistent.

4. Keep your answers brief and to the point, but not monosyllabic. An interview is a conversation, and you should keep up your end of it.

Questions the Interviewer Will Ask

Most questions interviewers ask fall into one of six categories.

Open-ended questions

- Tell me about yourself.
- Why should I hire you?
- What is it that you want to do?

These questions are of the fishing-expedition variety — the skilled interviewer wants to see what points you choose to bring up; the inexperienced interviewer may simply not know how to start with a better line of questioning.

For each question, decide what three to five points you want to get across. On the "tell me" question, you might say what you majored in and what subject you liked best at school and deliver a few sentences on what made you decide to go into this field or which job experiences have prepared you best for this job.

Questions about your interests

- Why do you want to work in this field (job, company)?
- What do you know about our company?
- Why did you major in _____?
- What is more important to you — the salary or the job itself?

If you have not had time to research the company in depth, make the point that it was because of the timing of the interview, not because you did not have time — and tell the interviewer what you do know and why you decided to interview with the company. Don't feel that you must apologize about your major if it is not the usual background for the job, but explain how you developed your interest in the area. If your interest in the job is primarily the kind of work itself, that's fine. But if other things — the location, size, or reputation of the company, or the opportunities for advancement — are also important, mention them, too.

Qualification questions

- What is your greatest strength? Weakness?
- Which two or three accomplishments have given you the most satisfaction? Why?
- What have your biggest disappointments been?

- What contributions could you make to this job (department, company)?
- How have you handled a major crisis or problem?

Watch out for these zingers. Concentrate on positive things, but don't exaggerate—the interviewer may figure he has an egomaniac on his hands and even check into inflated claims.

Be as specific as you can whenever possible and cite examples. Try to show how your abilities relate to the qualities the job calls for. If you have read a job description, however brief, zero in on the words mentioned there in forming answers. If the word "coordinate" or "organize" describes the job's responsibilities, you might mention your experience supervising a volunteer program on your campus. On the "major problem" question, find one that you resolved successfully or one that resulted from something positive—dealing with a group of angry citizens because of the petition drive you initiated to save a wildlife area in your community. When asked to reveal the sorrier aspects of your character, choose a "good" bad quality—your tendency to throw yourself into a project until it is done or your need to be around an action-packed office.

Questions about your goals

- What are your short-term and long-range goals?
- What do you expect to be doing in five years? ten years?
- How much would you like to be earning in five years?

Before you reveal your innermost fantasies, remember the interviewer is not a shrink, a counselor, or a friend. He wants to know whether you plan to make a serious commitment to the job or are more interested in experimenting with your career interests at his expense. Make sure your short-term goals are consistent with the scenario for a person in that job. Neither is it wise to say that five years from now you would like to be doing his job—or the company president's. That can sound too threatening—or downright naive. Instead, select a position to which you realistically could aspire. (Ditto for salary.) And, of course, it is not in your best interest to mention that what you eventually want to be is a ski bum. Dreams are best kept as secrets.

Personal questions

- What do you like to do in your free time?
- What books or magazines do you read?
- Are you willing to relocate; what is your geographic preference?
- What three people in public life do you most admire?

The motive behind these questions is to get answers that will cast additional light on you. (In the best of all possible worlds, an interviewer will share one of your passions.) Rather than mentioning an assortment of interests, single out one or two and make them work for you. If you are a runner, for example, and have successfully completed a marathon, mention that. It tells your employer that you are disciplined, competitive, and tenacious.

The single biggest problem campus recruiters have is talking job applicants into relocating, so if you are flexible about where you work, be sure to mention that.

Technical questions. If you are being interviewed by the person for whom you will be working or by a savvy recruiter, you may be asked questions that test your aptitude or your ability to think on your feet. There is not much you can do to prepare for technical questions; but if you are asked one to which you really do not know the answer, it is better to say so than to try to bluff your way through.

If you are asked a "what would you do in this situation" question, just answer it as best you can. Don't freeze if you can't give all the details; what the interviewer really is looking for is how resourceful and logical you are.

Illegal questions

- Your marital status (or plans)
- Your religious affiliation
- Whether you have children (how many, their ages), plan to, or are pregnant
- Whether you own or rent your home or apartment
- What your spouse or parents do
- Whether your spouse minds your working long hours or traveling
- What clubs or organizations you belong to
- Your date of birth or your age
- Whether you have AIDS or have tested positive for the AIDS virus
- Where you were born

Employers are not supposed to ask any of these, unless they relate specifically to your ability to do a job; but many still do, either out of ignorance or in the course of casual conversation. If you are asked an illegal question and you want the job, you have several options:

1. Answer it briefly if it seems innocent, but do not volunteer any additional information.

2. Answer the question, and if the employer seems concerned about its effect on your job performance reassure him. For example: "Yes, I am engaged, but I'll still be able to travel."

3. Give an indirect answer that accomplishes the same thing: "If what you are asking is would I be willing to relocate at a later time, yes, I would consider it."

4. Brush off the question with a light comment and a laugh, such as: "My career has top priority right now."

5. Remind him (without being accusatory, if you still want the job) that the question is illegal. "I'm surprised you ask that—I thought it was one of those off-limits questions in a job interview."

Questions You Should Ask

Interviewing the interviewer makes a lot of sense because you can:

- Learn more about the job or the company
- Find out what kind of boss he would be
- Show your interest in the company
- Communicate your interest and enthusiasm by asking his opinions and advice
- Get a better sense of what he's looking for in a job applicant and plan your later contacts accordingly

Save your most detailed questions for later interviews. Your potential boss-to-be is the person to ask about the downside of the job that may influence your decision—its tedious aspects, the extra hours or shifts you will be expected to put in, the risks of your not working out in the position.

Be sure to find out the answers to these questions before you make a decision:

- What exactly the job is—its title, responsibilities, the department or boss you would work for
- How the department job fits into the company structure—its purpose, its budget, the other departments with which it works
- Your opportunities for advancement
- Whether there have been any recent organizational shakeups
- What your predecessors in the job have moved on to
- Whether the position can be upgraded as your responsibilities grow
- How long the position has been open
- How job performance is measured

It is best not to bring up salary, fringe benefits, or "time-off" questions—let the interviewer bring up these topics. If he dodges the issue of salary by saying the company pays "the going rate," there's nothing wrong with trying to pin him down. Say that you've heard a wide range quoted, from $20,000 to $27,000 for example, and that you'd like to know where their salary range falls within that scale.

Eating Out: What to Do If the Interview Includes a Meal

You have made it through the first round of interviewing. The interviewer calls back to invite you for an all-day visit to the company, which includes lunch. Your table manners are no doubt considerably more civilized than the frat brothers' in *Animal House*, but you wish you could take an Emily Post refresher course in eating etiquette.

It is unusual for job candidates to be asked formal interview questions over lunch; employers mostly want to check out how well you handle yourself in public. That's especially true if the position requires your having to deal socially with clients.

For her callback interview with a major bank, Charlotte Meyer was invited to lunch in the executive dining room. She ordered kosher veal — it seemed like an inconspicuous enough choice. When the waiter brought the interviewer's appetizer, he began clearing away Charlotte's place setting. She tried to hide her confusion by continuing the conversation. When the entrees were served, Charlotte was given a paper bag that contained what looked like a picnic lunch — plastic flatware sealed in cellophane and food in a foil-covered box. (Kosher food is packaged to avoid contact with nonkosher food.) On top of all that, Charlotte didn't find the food appetizing. She sipped her water (and nearly died of embarrassment) while her interviewer ate. Despite her faux pas, Charlotte was hired, but that's no reason to take chances.

What to Order

The possibilities for dining slipups are numerous. Here are a few protective pointers:

1. Do not order a drink — mineral water is "in" anyhow. If the interviewer insists you join him, order one glass of wine and sip it slowly, no matter how many martinis he belts down. He can afford to be loose tongued; you cannot.

2. Avoid hard-to-control foods that may end up in your lap. Serious offenders are spaghetti (or anything with tomato sauce) and lobster.

3. Steer clear of garlic-seasoned dishes and foods like tunafish that leave an unpleasant afterbreath. You do not want to asphyxiate the people with whom you have afternoon interviews.

4. Do not order as if this were the first square meal you have had in weeks. If, on the other hand, you are too nervous to eat, ordering something light will prevent your having to spend an hour rearranging unwanted food on your plate.

5. Don't worry about expense. It's smart to avoid the most expensive items on the menu, but neither do you have to order a hamburger. The interviewer selected the restaurant and knows the price ranges.

What to Talk About

Mealtime conversation probably will be considerably more relaxed than even the small talk you made earlier. But certain things are worth keeping in mind:

1. Take conversational cues from the interviewer. Don't ask about his personal life, for example, unless he brings it up; and, even then, don't go too far.

2. Stick to neutral topics — food, sports, TV shows. Avoid, at all costs, politics and religion.

3. If your companions are recent graduates in their first jobs, feel free to ask their candid opinions about the company.

A Bad Interview: How to Get It Back on the Right Track

There are few things more depressing than leaving a job interview feeling that you've blown it. The first thing to realize is that your impression is no gauge of your chances of being hired. Some interviewers deadpan everyone they interview. Others are so encouraging that you wonder why you weren't offered the job on the spot.

A bad interview can as easily be the interviewer's fault as yours. He was in a bad mood; you were the twentieth person he saw that day; there were too many interruptions.

What if you get that sinking feeling while the interview is still going on? Sometimes an interview that takes a wrong turn can be put back on the track. Here's how to salvage the situation when the interviewer does any of the following:

Gets off the Topic

If your interviewer spends more than 5 minutes on something irrelevant, you might try to steer the conversation back by asking a job-related question.

Talks About Personal Problems

You may be a sympathetic listener and a captive audience, but this is not the time or the place. Plead a lack of expertise and ask a question about the job.

Acts Preoccupied

You may not be the main thing on his mind, but acting uninterested or not paying attention is downright rude. It's unlikely, though, that you can snap him out of his mood. Ask politely if he would rather reschedule the appointment at a more convenient time.

Makes You Conduct the Interview

The opening tell-me-about-yourself question may be his only one. If that is the case, be ready to take the initiative and explain why you want the job and what your qualifications are. The best way to activate this kind of interviewer is to ask him questions.

If you're absolutely certain after an interview that you were "off," call the interviewer and explain the circumstances. He may agree to schedule a second one. If you're sure the chemistry between you and the interviewer was completely wrong, it's better to wait until you get a rejection letter before you call up to ask if you might interview with someone else. After all, you have nothing to lose at this point except the time you spend making your request.

Follow-Up: It Can Make All the Difference

It took me years to pick up a simple rule of getting ahead — acknowledging people's help and interest. The most successful people I have met make it their business to thank others for favors, however small. It's smart to develop that habit early in your career. If the competition is close, a well-timed note can be a deciding factor in whether you're called back or even hired.

Your follow-up note need not be long. Try to mention something from the interview: "Your explanation of the differences between your training program and those of your competitors reinforced my feeling that your company offers the best opportunities for someone with my goals." (If you've interviewed with several people, don't send identical notes; that's insulting.) Don't summarize your qualifications for the job or go on at length about how terrific you think the company is — you may sound too hungry for the job.

Most employers will tell you when you can expect to hear from them about a further interview or whether you got the job. If they don't, ask. If you're not applying for a specific job opening, the interviewer may well give you the don't-call-us-we'll-call-you routine. Ask if he minds if you check back periodically. Make a phone call every two or three weeks (if it is a small business or turnover is light, you might want to make it every month so that you don't put him off with too frequent contact).

If you're really eager to work for an employer, persistence pays off. You may want to keep in touch even if you decide to take a job elsewhere. A personnel director at a manufacturing firm finally found a place for a business major who had called him every month for two years.

Rejection: How to Cope with It

Only 25 to 30 percent of those who interview on campus are asked back for a second interview. Most evaluations are extremely subjective. But interviewers agree on the main reasons that some candidates are dropped like hot potatoes:

- Personality problems — lack of self-confidence or too cocky; immature, no enthusiasm
- Lack of interest in the job or company
- Questionable work habits — not getting the job done, taking initiative, or being dependable

- Inadequate communication skills—inability to express ideas clearly

In most cases, it's impossible to figure out why you were not asked back or offered the job, so don't try. Rejection is easier to cope with if you:

1. *Keep your expectations in line.* Most interviews do not result in an offer. Your hopes may be more realistically raised if you thought a second or third interview went well. But even then, don't count on an offer—most employers, especially those who have plum openings, know that they can pick and choose from among a highly qualified group. Fewer than 10 percent of the students who interview with campus recruiters, for example, eventually begin working for those companies. If you keep that humbling statistic in mind, you should not be deterred when you get the big "NO." It is a lot easier to handle rejection if you chalk it up to "It was not meant to be, at least right now."

2. *Do not take the rejection personally.* You may have been rejected for reasons beyond your control—someone else had been hired unofficially, but the interviewer had to go through with the interview to satisfy company or government policies; or the interviewer found out after talking to you that budget restrictions would not allow him to replace the person who just left.

3. *Ask the interviewer for advice.* When you get that rejection letter or phone call, you shouldn't hesitate to call up the person who interviewed you. Ask if he can suggest anything that might help you on future job interviews or whether he knows of any other openings (at his company or others) that you might follow up on.

Evaluating a Job Offer: What to Consider Before You Accept

You got it—the letter or phone call offering you a job. Whether you get a handful of job offers or just one, don't rush right back with an answer. You don't have to worry about the employer rescinding his offer if you don't say yes immediately. Most employers prefer deliberation to hastiness—it's a sign that you're not planning to leave before he gets back his investment in your training.

Many first-job hunters pick salary as the main criterion in deciding whether to accept an offer. While how much you make is important (especially if you have financial obligations), a healthy paycheck won't cover your psychic-income deficit if you don't enjoy the work. The job itself should be your primary concern. If the day-to-day work is not appealing or you do not believe that working in that particular department or company will help you learn more about the field, you may find yourself looking for your second job sooner than you had anticipated.

A survey of college students found the following factors to be the most important in choosing their first jobs after graduation.

1. *The opportunities for promotion.* Seventy-three percent rated this factor as very important. How can you assess this job criterion? Ask how the job prepared its former holders for positions they moved on to—and whether they moved up within the company or left for another employer. Find out, too, how long you can anticipate staying in the job before you are given more responsibility.

2. *Job security.* Most college students (69 percent) want to feel that their long-term prospects for staying with an employer are good. In these times of corporate upheaval, there are, of course, no guarantees that the job you are hired for today will be there tomorrow. Still, before you take the job it's worth checking into whether belt-tightening is anticipated. And investigate how well or poorly the company handled cutbacks in the past.

3. *Long-term income potential.* A majority of the students (65 percent) want to feel that their efforts will be rewarded. Even if your starting salary is not enviable, find out whether hard-working professionals are well paid. For those who are working in the nonprofit sector, this factor is less critical. Still, you want to be sure you can make ends meet.

4. *The employee benefits package.* Sixty-three percent of the respondents rated this as an important consideration, as well it should be. In addition to health-care benefits, be sure to look at tuition reimbursement plans and any other fringe that is meaningful to you.

5. *Opportunities for exercising creativity or initiative.* More than half (61 percent) of the students felt strongly about this job factor. It's not easily measured, but you can get some sense of whether you will have such opportunities by asking your boss-to-be how your predecessor showed his creativity or initiative.

If you're weighing several offers, one of the best ways to compare them is to use the balance-sheet approach (see the section on "Decision Making" in Chapter 1).

If you didn't get a chance during your interviews for a close look at what you will be doing, where you will be working, and who your colleagues will be, find out now. It's better to know the disadvantages before you come on board. If your interview was after regular business hours, visit during the day. If the person you're replacing has been promoted, find him. He can give firsthand information about the pluses and minuses of the job.

Suppose you get a job offer from one employer while you're waiting to hear from another. Call the second employer, explain the situation, and ask about your status. If your scheduled interview with another employer hasn't taken place yet, ask the first employer when he needs an answer. If he can't wait, you can take the bird-in-hand position or the gambler's choice—turning Employer Number One down with the hunch that Employer Number Two will come through.

Suppose after several weeks of interviewing you get only one job offer, which you feel lukewarm about. Most of the time, you should resist the urge to accept it for the sake of having a job — you have, after all, been looking for only a short time. More offers should come your way if you keep looking or step up your job search. If you're feeling the pinch in your pocketbook, you may be better off taking a part-time or temporary job to get through the lean time and continue your job campaign.

If you've been looking for more than two months, and this is the first offer you've received, it could mean one of two things: you should lower your expectations and extend your search into related areas, or you haven't been using the right kind of (or enough) job-hunting strategies, and a reassessment is in order.

If the only entry-level job with a company is a secretarial slot, should you consider taking it to get your foot in the door?

Not if you're in a technical or policymaking field; it's simply too hard to jump the gap from clerical to professional. Other employers are divided on whether that move slows or dead-ends your advancement or helps you get where you want to be.

More employers are hiring college graduates into entry-level positions once filled by high school graduates because they are upgrading the position and feel that those with a four-year degree are better-equipped to do the job. The way to decide if taking such a position makes sense for you is to ask the interviewer these questions:

- Do most people who have had the job move on to better ones? How long does it take? (Early in my first job search I turned down a very promising job as a secretary on the staff of Children's Television Workshop because I didn't realize it was a stepping-stone job.)

- Are there other entry-level jobs available that might put you on a faster track? (If you suspect that an employer's entry-level jobs are sex-segregated, see Chapter 11, "Discrimination.")

- Will you be able to pick up skills on this job that will help you move up? If not, is there another low entry-level job that will teach you a specific skill?

- Is your boss willing to help you learn the business?

No matter how eager you are to start working, never accept an offer until you have received satisfactory answers to these questions and have taken the time to evaluate whether the situation is right for you.

6

Your First Job

*The Wall Street Shuffle: How to Adjust to a
Workday Routine . . . "Gofer" Tasks: Using
Them to Increase Your Responsibilities . . .
Office Etiquette: A Few Ground Rules . . .
Making Mistakes: How to Deal with the
Inevitable . . . Meeting Moxie: Getting Your
Ideas Accepted . . . A Professional Image: The
Fast Track to Getting Ahead . . . Getting
Reviewed: When to Expect Feedback and Raises*

It's official—you have started your first job. You have spent Day One happily filling out forms from the personnel office, taking a physical, being introduced to the people with whom you'll be working. On Day Two, you are told to update lists, proofread, type, run errands, order lunch for everyone else, cover the phones, or photocopy a stack of papers. You're in the army now. The only way to escape "grunt" status is to have some officer training—an advanced or technical degree—under your belt. And even if M.B.A.'s and J.D.'s don't get stuck with the menial tasks of liberal arts lackeys, they too get the jobs that no one else wants.

No matter how nicely your employer treated you before you were hired, brace yourself for the inevitable: you are a commodity in your employer's eyes, as expendable as a piece of office equipment. Like the adding machine, you are there to do a job. Newcomers who complain are resented; there are plenty of similarly qualified college grads who are willing to do the job—and keep their thoughts to themselves.

After getting his M.B.A. in accounting, Gary Ryan thought he would be working on tax return preparation with the partners of the Big Eight accounting firm that had hired him; instead, he did library research for the senior accountants, who were a notch above entry level.

Erlene Berry Wilson thought that as a news assistant at a TV station she would be helping to assign stories; she spent her first six months pulling copy off the wires and clipping newspaper articles.

When Todd Donahue signed on with a prestigious government agency, he figured he would play a role in making long-range educational policy decisions. After several months, he realized that his contribution was to put numbers into charts.

It's natural to have high expectations; after all, you've just spent four to seven years and a healthy amount of money preparing yourself for a career. But here's the hitch: your degree may have been valuable as a career entree; but no matter what kind it is, you can't coast into major responsibilities on it alone — you have got to prove yourself first. Proving yourself doesn't mean coming up with innovative ideas or solving problems no one else has been able to figure out. Before you can begin to offer even minor input, you will have to pay your dues — which usually means doing all the routine, boring, or unpleasant tasks no one else wants to do. (They did their share of it when they were in your shoes.)

In my first job as an editorial assistant, I was surprised that I was not included in staff meetings, that I was expected to do the "slave" labor in the department, and that I could not participate in the small amenities, like leaving early on vacation weekends, that everyone else on the staff took for granted. I learned quickly that my options were to grin and bear it or get out.

If you were a "star" in college or were lucky enough to land a fabulous short-term job, your expectations will take an even sharper nose dive.

As a college senior, Kate White had a starring role in a campus musical, earned academic honors, won a national magazine contest, and appeared on its cover. Six months after graduation, she was working as a secretary. When her boss told her, "We wash our own dishes around here," Kate thought she was speaking metaphorically, but in fact she was assigned kitchen clean-up duty after advertising luncheons.

Soon after he graduated, Joe Tabacco was hired as a temporary associate at a top law firm in Washington, D.C. He spent three months in a walnut-paneled office with a view of the courtyard, researching and writing the appeal brief for a convicted mass murderer. When he began working as a government trial attorney six months later, Joe spent several weeks filling out 2,500 document ID sheets. The windows in his office (which were permanently sealed shut) offered a panoramic view of nearby railroad yards.

If you want to keep your psyche intact, put your fantasies about being the next Jane Pauley or Steven Jobs on hold. The success stories in the media are featured simply because they're so rare. Most jobs, particularly first jobs, are pedestrian, banal, and tedious. That doesn't mean that you won't enjoy working — the change of pace from school, the new people, and team projects can be very exciting. But if you can't hold on to your fantasy of a first job being a dream job, you may feel like quitting the first week.

Here are the best ways to cope with status shock:

1. *Be flexible.* Even if you despise the work, develop a survival mind-set. A few weeks into your job, set up a game plan — where you want to be in six months, a year, and two years and what exactly you want to learn in that time. Having defined goals will help you get through the rough times when you are ready to trash your typewriter, throw your calculator out the window, or dump the day's work in the wastebasket.

2. *Develop humility.* Most success strategists stress the opposite, but they neglect to mention that arrogance can backfire unless you are a prodigy. Sure, you can't stand people treating you as if you don't know anything, but showing your resentment will get you nowhere. Better to be friendly, listen to their suggestions, and ask for their advice.

3. *Keep a low profile.* It is good to be seen and not heard, at least for the first few months. That doesn't mean you should be oblivious to what is going on around you; think of yourself as an infiltrator for a spy network — learn everything you can about the place, the people who work there, the way business is conducted.

Your first job will be critical in forming your job "personality" — how you solve problems, deal with people, sell your ideas. The sooner you recover from status shock, the more quickly you can be assimilated into the mainstream and find your own way to earning others' respect.

The Wall Street Shuffle: How to Adjust to a Workday Routine

One of the worst things about having a job — whether it is on Wall Street or Main Street — is having to show up every day at a prescribed time and having to stay there for 7 or 8 hours. There is no student union to hang out at between classes; in fact, the whole day can sometimes seem like one long, drawn-out lecture class. You can't break it up with tennis games or a snooze or with shooting the breeze with friends. Happy hours take place after hours. Welcome to the rat race.

The Graveyard Shift

In some businesses, being the new kid on the block means working at the least desirable times. If there are around-the-clock or weekend shifts, you will be assigned them — the 6 p.m. to 2 a.m. graveyard shifts on daily newspapers, the 11 p.m. to 7 a.m. shift of hospitals and manufacturers; the Friday-night and weekend hours at a retail store. That kind of schedule can crush your morale unless you adjust your life-style to the demands of your job.

"White Rabbit" Lateness

If you were always the last person into class, never wore a watch, and always kept your date waiting, now is the time to reform. Employers do not take kindly to tardiness, and unless your boss is the type who arrives well before the starting hour you will find yourself in the doghouse if you cruise in after him. Being late may seem a minor offense, but there are so few other ways for your boss to judge your performance early on that it becomes one of the main criteria. If you want to make a good impression, show up before you are expected to be there, even if it is to catch a bite of breakfast and read the paper.

It is also advisable not to leave at the stroke of quitting time. In many offices, meetings are often scheduled late in the day and spill over into nonworking hours. Even if you're not invited, you might hang around to take messages or find out if your boss needs help afterward. You can also learn a lot by sticking around after the majority of people clear out; managers and lower-level achieving types are likely to be around, and it is often a good time to chat informally.

Pay attention to the rhythm of the office to get a sense of when formal and informal work goes on. It pays to be around when things are happening, and that isn't always during normal working hours. If you're there you may be given something important to do that would otherwise be given to a higher-ranking staff member.

Developing a Desk Mentality

Even if you spent long hours in the school library booking it, you will not be prepared for the plight of the office worker: being a prisoner of your desk. Your work may require you to spend long periods of time typing, writing, drafting, drawing, or talking on the phone.

A desk job can be a mental and physical drag if you do not develop diversionary activities:

- Volunteer for any assignment that requires working with another department, doing library research, or running an errand outside the building.

- Strike up friendships with other people on your level who work in different departments. If your own responsibilities involve no one but your immediate boss, your only "out" from your desk is to take a conversation break.

- Try to get away from it all during your lunch hour. A half-hour squash game, a three-mile run, or an exercise class can relieve physical tension. If you work in a city, visit a museum, explore a neighborhood, take a picnic lunch to a park.

Taking Days Off

Even though you have a certain number of paid sick days, don't coddle yourself. Most bosses admire employees who show up when they are not feeling well, as long as their illness is not contagious. If you're the kind of person who rarely gets sick, taking an occasional mental health day is fine, provided you have been on the job at least six months. But it's better to say you are not feeling well than to admit you are ablebodied but need a break.

"Gofer" Tasks: Using Them to Increase Your Responsibilities

- The worst routine task Lucy Flynn encountered on her first job as administrative assistant to a city politician was taking his shirts to be starched by the local laundry.
- Even though his title was junior accountant, David Egan was expected to deliver the mail and pick up the coffee for the rest of the office.
- Frank Menson, a TV staff assistant, found out that the "assistant" part of his title meant making deliveries and running the copying machine.

Some first jobs include more menial work than others. You may feel it is degrading, beneath your dignity, or an insult to your intelligence and education, but employers consider it part of your training. The trick is to make the best of it, so that you do not become discouraged — and show it. If you prove you are indefatigable, better assignments will flow your way. Here's how:

1. *Take your responsibility seriously, no matter how trivial it seems.* One of my responsibilities on my first job was to keep all fifty of my boss's Eagle Mirado No. 2 pencils sharpened. I knew that my boss had a heavy editing hand; nonetheless, only Theodore Bernstein marking high school students' essays on "My Summer Vacation" could have gone through that many pencils in one day. So I allowed two thirds of the pencils to develop lead stubs before I sharpened them assembly-line style. After reminding me several times that I seemed to be shirking that responsibility, my boss called me in to say that it was important to her to have all the pencils sharp. My pencil-sharpening skills improved.

2. *Maintain your sense of humor.* It may be hard to keep smiling when you have spent long hours doing a rote task. But making a joke about it releases your feelings; it's one of the best ways to get through the junk work with your self-respect intact and to keep other people from feeling they are asking a big favor of you.

3. *Make the work important.* Extra effort can make the difference between something that's routine and a chance to show your stuff. Joe Tabacco did just that when his boss handed him a complaint letter that other lawyers at the U.S. Department of Justice did not think was worth pursuing. Joe thoroughly researched the case, which involved price fixing; on the basis of his recommendations, the case was referred to the attorney general for prosecution.

4. *Volunteer to do jobs no one else wants to do.* People who are willing to get their hands dirty go a lot farther than prima donnas. After he was on the job for a week, Roger Turnes offered to come in on Saturday to help his supervisor through a crisis period. He had not been around long enough to know how to do anything more than run errands, but he was

able to pick up a lot from watching more experienced engineers work, and he made a great impression on his boss.

Volunteering to help out someone other than your boss is fine, too; it's a good way to learn how to do things you ordinarily would not get a chance to do, and the people you help out are likely to return the favor when they get the chance. Be sure to check with your boss before you offer.

Office Etiquette: A Few Ground Rules

Nothing can get you into hot water faster than violating one of the unwritten rules of your department or company. It's unlikely that anyone will bother to tell you what they are — you simply have to pick them up by observing other people.

Here are some general guidelines that should help you avoid making the most obvious blunders, but you will have to learn those peculiar to your office.

Phone Manners

When you were in college, you may have answered your phone "We deliver," "Joe's Bar and Grill," or "Casey's Cathouse," but anything less than serious is taboo in the business world. If you are responsible for picking up your boss's lines (or others), ask how he would prefer you to identify him — or the office.

Always ask who is calling (never: "Who is this?" always: "May I ask who is calling?"), and get the name straight. Bosses always like to have a minute to collect themselves for business calls. If you do not recognize the name, ask what the person is calling in reference to; your boss may want you to handle less important calls. If you have to put the caller on hold, make sure he cannot hear the exchange between you and your boss; you can jeopardize a business deal or relationship. If your boss is not in, don't give the caller the specifics (e.g., "He is playing tennis right now"); just ask whether there's a message.

If your boss is on another line, determine how important the call is before you interrupt him. If it is one of his bosses, always interrupt. (A phone call from an important client, a call from someone he has been trying to reach, and a call from his immediate family usually warrant interruptions.) If you are not sure, writing a note is the least obtrusive way to check.

Even if covering the phones is not your favorite task, don't let any feelings of resentment creep into your voice. You never know when the person on the other end is someone important who may compliment you to your boss or complain to him about the way you treated him.

If you answer your own phone, it is usually best to follow the protocol in the office. If you use your name, say, "Hello, this is [your name]," or simply, "[your name]." Never just say, "Hello." The caller will have to ask if he has the right company and whether you're the person he's trying to reach.

Finally, keep the following things in mind when you are making or taking a call:

- Make yourself sound important by speaking clearly and self-confidently. If necessary, rehearse what you are going to say ahead of time so that you don't trip over your own words.
- Always identify yourself and your company.
- Get to the point of your call right away — many people prefer straight business calls to those filled with weather commentaries and small talk.
- Modulate your voice so that the person on the other end does not have to strain to hear you or keep the receiver 3 inches away from his ear. Few things will make you more unpopular among your nearby coworkers than a loud telephone voice.

What to Call Your Boss, Coworkers, Clients

How you address the people you work with — and your supervisors — depends on how formal the company is.

Your boss probably will tell you what he prefers to be called; if he does not, ask. It is a good idea, though, to address his supervisors by their last names, at least until you get to know them and they tell you to call them by their first names or you see that your colleagues do.

Although you may have a tough time calling a coworker your mother's age by her first name, if that's what everyone else calls her she probably will feel more comfortable if you do.

Even though you (and the other professionals in your department) may be on a first-name basis with your boss, you may be expected to refer to him as Mr. (his name) when you are talking about him with people on a different job level — clerical or support staff people. When you are taking a call for him, always refer to him by his last name, unless, of course, the caller is a good personal friend.

Making Mistakes: How to Deal with the Inevitable

You blew it. You feel badly about the mistake, and the fact that your boss is upset makes it even worse. You're wondering if it means curtains for your career — or at least this job. That, you will be comforted to know, rarely happens unless your mistake costs the company big bucks, major embarrassment, or a legal jam.

It's inevitable that you will find yourself in a pickle early into your first job — the opportunities for beginners' errors are numerous. Making a mistake is one of those things you have to be philosophical about, because it's going to happen again. The more experienced you are, the bigger your mistakes will be—and the less sympathy you will get. The other thing to keep in mind is that everybody fouls up once in a while. And the most innovative people usually have the worst track records, because they take risks.

Mistakes fall into different categories, some of which are more excusable than others.

The Careless Mistake

This variety occurs when you are doing rote work. One of Leslie Thompson Williams's responsibilities as sales coordinator for a TV station was to log in the name and length of commercials so that they could be aired in the correct order. Advertisers pay big money to get their commercials in the right time spots and they are irate when there is a mix-up, a fact Leslie quickly became aware of after a few minor slipups.

The Honest Mistake

Tim Hayes, who worked for a government agency, took home some raw data to work on without having made copies and inadvertently left the papers on a bus. He chased the bus and checked with transit headquarters, but the papers were gone. He was a basket case when he told his boss the next day. Even though it was a real loss, his boss went easy on the criticism because Tim had done everything he could to find the papers and clearly didn't take his error lightly.

The Innocent Mistake

This is the one you made because you didn't have experience enough to know that it was the wrong thing to do. Mistakes that fall into this category include foot-in-mouth problems, usually caused when you decide to put in your two cents worth to a client or someone who matters and reveal confidences or information that was better left unsaid; or the unauthorized phone call or letter, the result of not wanting to disturb your boss.

The Stupid Mistake

Slips of this type should not ever happen, but they do—and they really make you look and feel like a jerk. A recent college graduate who had been working for several months at a TV station put the word "Gorbachef" on a character generator, the device that projects lettering on the screen. There is no way to defend these mistakes; you simply have to take the rap, act contrite, and not ever make a similar slipup again.

If you make a mistake that no one except you is immediately aware of, it usually is best to alert your boss or whomever it will affect—they might be able to rectify it or assure you that it is not so disastrous as you imagined. There is nothing wrong with camouflaging a mistake, but, if it's bound to come out eventually, it's best to own up to it. Sure you may get bawled out, but keep one thing in mind: learning how to deal with criticism is a skill worth developing early in your career. Make sure you understand what you did wrong, so that you don't make the same error again.

Once a mistake is over and done with, forget about it — there is nothing to be gained from obsessing about what you might have done. It's all right to make every mistake in the book on your first job; but it's just not smart to make the same mistake twice.

Meeting Moxie: Getting Your Ideas Accepted

Whether you will be invited to meetings soon after you start depends on the protocol in your department and whether the subject matter of the meeting directly affects your work. Don't take it personally if you're not included; find out when newcomers are asked by talking with someone who's been there awhile.

It was six months before I was permitted to attend an editorial meeting where ideas for upcoming articles were discussed. The second week on the job, I told my boss I had ideas and asked whether I could attend. The answer was no — I was expected to cover the phones. So I submitted formal article proposals; none of my ideas was accepted, but my boss was impressed with my enthusiasm, and I was eventually invited to present them at the meeting itself.

When you are given the go-ahead to attend staff meetings, be sure to come prepared. Know what is going to be discussed and what kinds of suggestions would be most helpful. Research your ideas beforehand — get facts, figures, whatever you need to back up your statements. Talk over your ideas with others in your office — they can give you valuable feedback and bring up objections that might come up at the meeting.

Here are some pointers on how to present your ideas in a meeting:

- Do not say, "This might not work, but . . . ," or, "This may be a lousy idea, but. . . ." Be positive. If you're not enthusiastic about your idea, no one else is likely to be.
- Make a list of points you want to bring up; that way you will be able to articulate your idea effectively, and you won't leave out anything vital.
- Don't go off on a tangent or give unnecessary background (e.g., "This idea came to me the other night after I had dinner with my cousin."). Be concise and to the point.
- Avoid references to your personal stake in the idea. It is less likely to be accepted if it seems too self-serving.
- If no one asks you for your ideas, do whatever is necessary to get your turn. Raise your hand, stand up, or say, "Excuse me, but I would like to say something, too."
- Develop a fallback position in the event that your initial presentation is shot down. Flexibility is the key to getting your ideas accepted.

- Try to enlist the support of others in the group by showing how your idea complements one they brought up earlier, or how the two ideas might be combined to form an even better plan.

You should not feel that you have to make major contributions during your first few meetings, although it is to your credit to come prepared with some thoughts. Pay attention to who takes control in the meeting, which kind of ideas are warmly received, and how they are presented. Note what is accomplished and what isn't. Not all meetings are productive; it may take several sessions to resolve a seemingly minor problem. Other meetings are called less to brainstorm then to hear one person (usually the boss) pontificate. Make sure that bringing up the topic you have prepared isn't out of line; if the meeting never gets past issue one, shelve your idea until the next time.

After the meeting, it is helpful to talk to someone who attends regularly to get a reading on whether you interpreted things correctly or why certain decisions were made.

A Professional Image: The Fast Track to Getting Ahead

The most important element in getting ahead is projecting a professional image. Your boss and others in management need to believe that you have the maturity to make judgments, work well with others, and get the job done. In fact, in your first job those qualities are more important than your technical know-how.

It took me the better part of Job One to develop any semblance of professionalism. I figured my talent would speak for itself; I simply did not have the savvy to know that the extras — my appearance, behavior, way of speaking — were crucial to being taken seriously. I assumed incorrectly that people at work would be as sensitive to my potential as my professors in college had been. But you cannot expect that simply doing a competent or even an excellent job will gain the notice of anyone except perhaps your immediate superior. You will at first be judged, perhaps, on things that are not work related at all — on the way you handle yourself and what you say.

When, some years later, I was in a quandary over which of two equally qualified recent college graduates to hire as my assistant, I finally went with the one I felt had "presence." She was the kind of person who immediately inspired confidence, and since part of her job would involve dealing with people much older than herself, I felt she was a step ahead of the other candidate who still had not shed her student persona.

The college-to-career transition is easy for a few take-charge types. For most recent grads, that's a quality that takes work to acquire. Here is what successful college graduates and employers say are the most important components in projecting a professional image:

Dress the Part
Even if you work in a place where casual clothing is acceptable or where all of your peers dress more casually than their seniors, pattern your wardrobe after the people to whose jobs you aspire. You obviously will not be able to match labels with them, but you can put together an equally polished look without putting out big bucks.

Know How to Take Criticism
You spent the better part of the last two weeks laboring over a proposal you were assigned. You turn it in, feeling it is truly your best effort. When it comes back to you later that day, you're devastated. There are more red marks on it than there were on all your term papers combined. Before you conclude that your failure to meet the standards of a final product on your first draft points to gross incompetence, consider this: it is a lot easier to critique something than it is to come up with the original ideas, and your boss has had significantly more practice in doing both. No one, not even the best and the brightest, gets his efforts approved without changes, which, for the first few months, are usually significant.

It is a good idea to separate your ego from your work early on—if you don't, people will find it hard to deal with you honestly without offending you, and you will never learn how to improve. When your work is criticized (regardless of the tone of voice in which it is done), avoid getting defensive or reacting emotionally. If you feel upset, take a walk to compose yourself. If you do not understand what you did wrong, ask. Throw out a few new ideas to see if you are on the right track. And then head back to the drawing board without complaint—even if it is your fifth attempt.

Learn How to Set Priorities
You have three things to get done by the end of the week, but now there's an even bigger emergency. Which assignment gets put off? At first, you will simply have to ask your boss or someone more experienced what work takes priority. As you catch on to the flow of work, you will get more assignments: people will see that you can juggle successfully.

Some employers even test your sense of priorities. Michael Husar, a senior engineer and group leader at a General Motors plant, sometimes gave conflicting responsibilities to newly hired engineers. The main assignment might be troubleshooting the assembly line, for example, and the special request an engineering task with a deadline. When the line goes down because of a problem, does the engineer solve it, or does he rely on the line people to handle it themselves because he is involved in more "interesting" work? It's always more important to take care of your primary responsibility even if you don't think it's as important as your special assignment. If something goes wrong because of your neglect, you may not be given special assignments in the future.

Meet Deadlines

Employers say that one of the main reasons interns and law clerks are not "asked back" is that they did not finish a project on time—or do a thorough job. You may not always be aware of the importance of doing a particular assignment promptly, but it may be crucial to your boss. So hop to it, unless your boss tells you that he does not need it right away.

Develop Visibility

Once you know your way around the place, it's smart to make sure that important people get to know who you are. That can be hard if you work for one person. Make yourself seen—hand-deliver memos from your boss to the head honcho, for example. After people get used to seeing you around, you can start making yourself heard too. You might tacк a positive comment onto a "Hello"—"The project you're working on with my boss seems really exciting." It's not a good idea to give suggestions or your opinion unless you're asked; on the other hand, showing that you're aware of things outside of your job lets others know that you're really plugged in.

Present Useful Ideas

Few things are considered more obnoxious by employers than a rookie who tells them what they're doing wrong or how things could be improved. The probability is that it's been thought of already (and discarded because it was impractical) or tried and found unworkable. For at least the first few months, limit your suggestions to ways of improving how you do your job.

After you have had a chance to observe the various needs (or inefficiencies) in your office, it's fine to make a suggestion. But first find out whether it's been tried before. Be ready to explain how your proposal will save time or money or generate new business. Even if your suggestion does not involve your boss directly, always check it out with him first.

Act Self-Confident

If you want to earn respect, it's important to act as if you know what you're doing even if you don't entirely. Self-confident behavior includes speaking clearly and loud enough to be heard, maintaining eye contact with the person you are talking to, not appearing rattled when you are doing something for the first time; taking pressure in stride. But make sure your self-confidence does not come across as cockiness.

Don't Talk Too Often About College Days

It is smart to keep your tales of school for more appreciative audiences. Most people at work don't care about what you did in college. The faster you shed your student identity, the more easily you will fit into your office.

Getting Reviewed: When to Expect Feedback and Raises

In many companies, your paycheck is the closest thing you will get to feedback. It doesn't occur to most bosses to tell you when you're doing fine; they only flag you when you goof. If your boss corrects you twenty-five times during your first six months on the job and never compliments you once, you may feel like a failure. That is seldom the case.

Most employers do not expect much from recent college grads during their first few months. They realize it takes time to acclimate and to learn the routine. Nonetheless, your first six months are a trial period, during which time your employer is assessing your strengths and weaknesses and whether you're going to make it in this job. How is your performance judged during this time? Many judgments are made on the basis of things you may feel are inconsequential, harmless, or even meaningless. If you are guilty of any of the offenses below, however, your employer's opinion of you may sink faster than a barometer when a thunderstorm approaches:

- *A disorganized desk.* It does not matter how sloppy your boss's office is. If your desk or work area is constantly in a shambles, the conclusion your boss will draw is that you are not an organized person.

- *Too many personal phone calls.* Keep the number and length of calls to a minimum especially if you are within earshot of your boss. Otherwise you will give the impression that you do not care about work or that you do not have enough to do.

- *Socializing too often with your coworkers.* Shooting the breeze may have been one of your favorite pastimes in college, but it does not have much place during working hours, except when you are taking a break.

- *Goofing off.* Murphy's Law (if anything can go wrong, it will) operates here. The minute you slough off propriety or start clowning around is the time the boss will come by. That is what happened to Bob Allen, who managed the toy department of a large department store. He had been placing a toy ray gun into a display, but since business was slow, he started playing with it. Just then, the chairman of the board rode up the escalator. He said nothing, but Bob knew he had seen the whole thing.

Your boss may not mention anything specific to you about this sort of behavior unless it is really out of line, but the impression such slipups leave will affect you in ways you may not realize. He may decide, for example, to give more challenging work to another newcomer who has acted more responsibly.

If you are in a formal training program, you probably will get a great deal of feedback during your first six months on the job. The person assigned to train you really is acting in the capacity of teacher, which makes it easier to critique your performance. Learning the ropes in a more structured way lends itself to a dialogue about "How am I doing?"

For those getting regular informal appraisals, the idea of being formally reviewed is much less traumatic than it is for the majority of people in their first job. In companies with a formal evaluation policy (usually the case with big corporations), you probably will be reviewed six to eight months after you are on the job. Some personnel departments require supervisors to fill out elaborate evaluation forms that rate everything from your technical know-how to how well you get along with your coworkers. After your boss has filled it out, you are sent a copy and the two of you sit down and discuss the ratings. Don't be disappointed if you do not get a rave review the first time. Your boss may feel that you're capable of even more, and this is his way of encouraging you to try harder. Or he simply may not want to overreward you this soon because you might develop an easy-street attitude.

If you got a good review, you probably will be given a raise. During your first eighteen months, raises are likely to be small, but they're given more frequently than they are to higher-salaried employees. That's because salaries for most entry-level employees are at the low end of the range for their job. The closer you get to the top of the range, the longer the interval between raises: exceeding the salary range for your job throws off the payroll budget — only a promotion to a job with a higher range can relieve that situation.

Privately owned companies and those that employ fewer than 500 people usually have much more informal review systems; their workings are often so mysterious, in fact, that you may have to bring up the subject yourself. Often a review is important to you because it ties into a raise. Just before the Christmas-rush season, Carolyn Egan took over as manager of a clothing boutique (she had been hired as assistant manager six months before). Two months later, Carolyn finally brought up the subject of a raise with her supervisor. She told him that she knew the former manager made $5,000 more than she did, and that she felt she deserved at least half that amount because of her success during the Christmas season. A week later, her supervisor offered her a $1,000 raise. She told him that wasn't enough and left after training a new manager. In retrospect, Carolyn feels she could have done better; putting a dollar amount on the raise she thought she deserved boxed in her employer, and comparing herself to the former manager put him on the defensive.

The best way to broach the subject of a raise is to ask for a review of your work. You can get some useful tips from your coworkers by asking them what their experiences have been and whether initiating the subject would be out of line. If it isn't, enumerate the reasons that you feel you deserve a raise before you talk to your boss.

It may be difficult to point to anything specific you have accomplished (although that is the kind of ammunition to use when you have been working longer). Instead, talk about the things you have learned and the times you voluntarily worked late or helped out.

In later reviews, how well you do your job will count as much as or more than your behavior and attitude. How well you get along with other people, though, will continue to be important, and your boss also will assess how well you handle crises or new situations, what you have contributed beyond what your job description calls for, and how quickly you pick up and use information.

7

Bosses

The Hard, Cold Facts . . . Boss Types: Tuning In to Your Boss's Personality and Work Style . . . The Most Common Boss Problems: How to Handle Them . . . A Good Relationship with Your Boss: How to Develop One . . . Women Bosses: Advice for Men . . . Socializing with Your Boss: The Unwritten Rules . . . Mentors: How They Can Give Your Career a Boost

The Hard, Cold Facts

- Your boss won't always look out for you. He (or she, as the case may be) looks out first for himself, then for the company. If you're lucky, you're third on the list.
- Every boss has pet peeves. They rarely make sense to anyone but him, but no matter.
- Your boss isn't your professor. Or your parent. Or your older sister. You won't get graded; chances are, you won't get praised either. The only time you can count on getting feedback is when you do something wrong.
- Most bosses don't know their own weaknesses. Whether or not they do, though, they don't want to hear about them from an underling.
- If your boss is having a bad day, he can let it show, or even take it out on you. If you do that, you can get fired.
- Your boss isn't necessarily interested in promoting you. He's interested in promoting himself. Therefore, what helps him will probably help you.

87

- Even if your boss gets away with murder, that doesn't mean you can.
- Bosses are not above taking credit for your work and ideas. Beware.
- Bosses don't like competition from their employees. If you're smarter than he is, keep it to yourself.
- Nine times out of ten, your boss won't explain why he wants something done (or done in a particular way). Any bright, ambitious employee should be selective about asking, "Why?"

You've probably worked for a number of bosses already—a college professor as disorganized with his paperwork as he was brilliant in class, a camp director who liked to play drill sergeant, a fast-food manager who cared more about hamburgers than about you. The relationships you develop on your first "real" job probably will be more formal, and, because you will have more at stake, you'll want to be more cautious about how you act.

The best definition of "boss" I've come across is: "The person who can get you a raise by checking with only one other person and who can fire you without checking with anyone." To that I would add: "A boss is someone who determines whether—and how fast—you move up and who can make your life miserable if your relationship sours."

Boss Types: Tuning In to Your Boss's Personality and Work Style

It's useful to understand the kind of person your boss is and how he works, for these reasons:

1. You will be able to prevent friction and will work more efficiently.

2. You will be a step ahead of your peers who don't take mental notes on how their boss works.

3. Knowing what makes a boss effective or incompetent will help you develop your own management skills.

The Climber

Aggressive, upwardly mobile, and often ruthless in the pursuit of his ambitions (he calls them "company goals"), the Climber is far more interested in what his employees can do for him than vice versa. He knows how to look out for himself, and chances are that he'll look out for you, too, if you make yourself invaluable to him. The Climber keeps his personal life out of the office (and he expects you to do likewise); he can't afford to have it interfere—or have others think it does. He'll make the decisions, set the goals, solve the problems; he may resent your attempts to get involved in any activities but those he can't be bothered with.

The Automaton

Security and order are the primary concerns of the Automaton, who is usually an up-through-the-ranks employee. He has loyally and faithfully carried out others' directions and has been rewarded with big responsibilities. Unfortunately, he doesn't know how to deal with them. The Automaton is not particularly open to change and often resents a young, bright subordinate. You will get along with him if you come across as enthusiastic rather than ambitious. Keep your eyes fixed from Day One on other horizons, so that once you've learned all you can from him you can move on to a boss who can teach you more.

The Pleaser

The Pleaser is concerned with keeping his "people" happy — what others think of him matters a great deal. He is like your introductory psych professor who spent more time telling entertaining case histories than explaining substance. It's easy and often enjoyable to work for a Pleaser, but you may not learn much — he hates to criticize, even constructively; he is more of a backslapper than a diplomat. The Pleaser's greatest weakness is his inability to deal with, or even to admit to, painful realities — problems that must be solved, changes that must be made, people who aren't competent. While he is usually more adventurous than the Automaton, the Pleaser will stop short of taking on a challenge if it will jeopardize his personal relationships. The danger of working for a Pleaser is that you may become too comfortable and stay too long.

The Loner

He may be brilliant, a real mover and shaker. Or he may not care about his work and turn in a maintenance-level performance. In either case, what makes working for the Loner difficult is his absorption in his own problems. The Loner is cool, individualistic, and distant — he's as difficult to tune in as a good radio station late on a Sunday night, when all the public service broadcasting is on. You'll be left to your own resources much of the time, which can be rough when you're starting out. Don't hesitate to develop contacts with other people who are willing to spend more time teaching you. But be discreet.

The Coach

The most balanced of the types, the Coach cares about his work, keeps the company's goals in perspective, and is interested in you, your job satisfaction, and your progress. He's not afraid to give criticism — or to get it. He encourages questions and discussion, and when it's relevant to their work he lets the people who work for him in on the reasons behind decisions. The Coach delegates authority to people he thinks can handle it and doesn't mind your taking the initiative if you know what you're doing. When it's time for you to go on to a better job, he'll probably be the first to help you make the move.

Tuning in to your boss's work style can save you untold aggravation. Being sensitive to how he likes things done makes handling his requests much easier. One of the key elements of your boss's work style is how he likes to get information. Management expert Peter Drucker divides bosses into two groups: readers and listeners. Readers like to be handed written information — they can comprehend ideas better that way. Listeners prefer to hear the message — that gives them a chance to ask questions and clarify points right away. If your boss doesn't tell you what approach he prefers, try both to see which one he is more responsive to.

How much your boss wants to know is important to determine, too. Some bosses want only the overview — if they're excited by an idea and think it's reasonable, they want you to worry about how to execute it. The "details" boss, on the other hand, wants to know not only what and why but also a great deal of how. If you're asked to research something, it's usually a good idea to give your boss more than he asked for. But be careful to keep the main points clear so that he doesn't have to search through the material to find what he asked for.

Bosses also differ in how involved they like to be in your work. The Automaton appreciates being kept posted on even the smallest of details to reassure him everything is under control. The Loner is content to know that the project you're working on is coming along fine. Your boss may be somewhere in between. It's good to find out just where.

Some "good news" bosses, for instance, don't like to hear about problems. But if you cannot solve something on your own (or with the advice of more experienced coworkers), let your boss know. He will probably learn about it anyway, and it's better if he hears about it from you.

Observing your boss's work style does more than help the two of you get along better; it can help you start developing management qualities of your own. I made an important discovery watching my first two bosses work their way into top management positions: that there are different ways to get to the top.

What kinds of boss behavior are important to observe? Here is a list of twenty items worth noticing. How your boss:

1. Schedules a busy day
2. Delegates responsibility
3. Develops plans and strategies
4. Conducts a meeting
5. Gets an idea accepted at a meeting
6. Gives and takes criticism
7. Rejects someone else's idea or plan
8. Gets his boss to see his point of view
9. Decides which plan (product, idea) to go with
10. Makes a successful sales call
11. Deals with a complaint from an employee or client
12. Persuades people to do things his way
13. Treats people who aren't in a position to help him
14. Researches information or problems
15. Works under pressure
16. Handles being confronted with a mistake an employee has made

17. Acts when angry
18. Apologizes
19. Brings up sensitive issues
20. Fires someone

You'll get a lot of this information from simply watching your boss and paying attention to letters, memos, and conversations. The only way to find out other things — why your boss decided on the red packaging instead of the blue, for instance — is to ask. There are no rules about what questions to ask and when to ask them. If you put yourself in your boss's shoes, you'll be better able to judge when a question is too personal or too sensitive and what the right timing is.

The Most Common Boss Problems: How to Handle Them

Everyone from the mailroom clerk to the president of a Fortune 500 company has boss problems. These problems weren't likely to surface the first day or even the first week you were on the job; you'll no doubt enjoy what is referred to in the working world as a "honeymoon" period of several weeks. That term seemed to me to be an odd way to describe a work situation until I realized after working for a few years that the boss-employee relationship is like a romance in some ways, even if the sexes aren't opposite. Getting the silent treatment, acting defensively, saying things you don't mean, walking out can happen to either of you. And as it often is with romantic relationships, how your boss treats you may have less to do with your behavior or performance than it does with other pressures in his life.

And that, I discovered after several unsettling experiences, is good to keep in mind, since you can develop ulcers at an early age if you take things too personally. It's easy to say you shouldn't let your boss's off-hand comment get to you, hard to convince yourself he really didn't mean to be so harsh. But if you find that office scenarios starring your boss as antagonist are playing on your mind as often as soap operas on afternoon TV, it's a sure bet you're overinvolved in the relationship.

The most consoling thought when life with your boss is at an all-time low is that you're not the first person to feel that way.

Here are some of the most common boss problems for first-time employees. If there's a bottom-line solution they all have in common, it's this: you waste more time and energy bottling up your frustrations than by asserting yourself.

Personal Favors

Should you do personal favors for your boss? It depends on:

1. *How big the favor is.* If it won't take much time or effort, it's probably easier to do it than to refuse. If it is time-consuming or cuts into your free

time, it may be worth doing if your boss is in a pinch or if he offers to reimburse you for your time and trouble and the deal strikes you as fair.

2. *How often he asks.* If personal favors are becoming a regular part of your job, your best approach may be to say lightly that those tasks weren't included in your job description when you were hired. If your boss rarely asks favors, it's in your best interest to be flexible.

3. *Whether others on your level are asked to do similar favors.* Women are more apt than men to be asked to run personal errands for their bosses. You may do yourself a disservice by doing what men on your level aren't asked to do—or won't do. If, on the other hand, the practice is an accepted one in your office, you may get flak from your boss if you aren't cooperative.

If you decide to confront your boss, and if you also care about keeping your job, the best approach is to discuss the matter with him rather than to refuse outright to grant his request. In large companies, official policy may back you up.

The Boss Who's Too Busy

It's the mover-and-shaker boss who is most prone to the butterfly syndrome. He flits from a phone call to a meeting to a luncheon appointment—he's too elusive to be pinned down or puts off your questions or problems with a "Later" or a "Can't you handle that?"

If you're just starting out, you may feel insecure about going ahead on your own. And justifiably—without enough information you could make a serious mistake; almost as bad, you might assume more responsibility than your boss intended you to have. No matter how resourceful you are, there will be times when you need your boss's guidance. If you're unsure of where your responsibilities begin and end, have a discussion with your boss.

If pinning him down on important matters continues to be a problem after you talk about it, suggest scheduling a set, if brief, time every few days for the two of you to go over any problems you're having.

Working for a Tyrant

On the day Michael Simon started work, a snowstorm hit. He was supposed to be on the job at 8 a.m., but even though he left home early he didn't get to the office until 8:03. Mike was embarrassed when his boss called his name over the intercom and asked him to come to his office. He told Mike that if he wasn't in at 8 in the future he shouldn't bother coming in at all. The incident let Mike know very clearly what he was in for.

A boss who is a tyrant rules by intimidation: he uses insults, treats you like a child, bawls you out in front of others, or screams at you to assert his power. The first few months may be particularly rough because a tyrannical boss wants to whip you into shape. You'll probably feel like quitting on many occasions, but if your boss is respected for his work it will probably pay to stick around and learn from him. The challenge is to develop ways to successfully manage your relationship with him. John O'Hara worked for a classic despot, a man with an imperious personality, considered one of the shrewdest dealers in his business. John took his daily dose of reprimands for a while, but when his boss didn't let up John told him he didn't deserve that kind of abuse. Although his boss continued to criticize him, his attacks became less personal.

The best way to keep your sanity if you work for a tyrant is to dig a mental Grand Canyon between your personal feelings and your professional relationship. Then try to switch your attention from your boss's personal idiosyncrasies to his professional strengths. Tune out the things he says or does that don't involve you or your work. Keep in mind that what really counts is what you're learning and doing on the job. And look at it this way: if your first boss is a nut and you get what you want, coping with future bosses will be a cinch.

When You Don't Get Enough Feedback

One of the hardest things to get used to when you're starting your first job is not getting regular feedback.

Many bosses are reluctant to give criticism or praise; they react only when you make a mistake so serious it puts them on the line. Why? Some (especially the Climber, the Automaton, and the Loner) feel that giving praise costs them a loss of authority. Others hold back because they've seen some employees turn a mild compliment into unrealistic expectations. Some bosses are equally unwilling to criticize constructively. Some find it easier to redo a job themselves and figure you'll pick up on your mistakes if you see how they've done it (that's often very difficult to do). Some bosses (especially the Pleaser variety) can't bring themselves to criticize because they don't want to hurt your feelings, which is ultimately to your disadvantage.

So what can you do about the boss who gives too little feedback? Tell your boss that you're interested in improving. Mention ideas you've thought of or have already incorporated into your work and then ask for suggestions. Using tact is better than asking your boss point-blank about your performance; the conversation will be easier for both of you, and you're likely to come away with a better idea of each other's needs and expectations. You may find out that your boss appreciates your work a lot more than you realized.

Disagreeing with Your Boss

It's not, generally, a good idea to disagree with your boss:

- Once a decision has been made
- When nothing is accomplished other than making your boss feel guilty (in the event that he really did make a mistake and knows it)

Appropriate times to disagree with your boss are:

- When either you or your work has been misrepresented or compromised

- When there's still enough time to correct or change the situation
- If the matter is likely to come up again

How well and how diplomatically you articulate your disagreement may ultimately determine how pleased you'll be with the outcome. (Remember, your boss has an ego, too, and you can lose your case if you make him look stupid.) One good tactic is to phrase your disagreement so that it sounds as if you're primarily concerned with your boss's and/or your company's interests: "If we handled the project this way, we could reduce the costs." It's definitively a plus if you can present several alternatives, ideally ones that incorporate your boss's thinking or earlier suggestions.

No matter how strongly you may feel about an issue, it's in your best interest to play it cool. If things don't turn out the way you'd hoped, take a walk, meditate, or buy yourself some new clothing—but don't show your irritation or disappointment. When my boss decided to cut several sections I considered essential to a piece, I walked back to my office, threw my papers across the room, and went for a walk. I disagreed fiercely with my boss's reasons. But I also realized the most important thing of all: she was the boss, not I. An hour later, I returned to my office, picked up the papers, and began a rewrite. I wasn't any happier about her decision, but at least I could work without being distracted by my feelings.

One of the worst sins or insubordination is to go over your boss's head when you disagree with him or don't think he will go along with a request. If you're tempted to bypass your boss, know the following:

1. You should always talk to him first, whether or not you respect his judgment, whether or not you suspect he's going to be against your idea, and regardless of how well you get along. That way, if you do decide to take your case to a higher power, you can at least say that you tried.

2. It's generally dangerous to go over your boss's head if he gets along well with the person you're planning to go to or is highly regarded by management. No matter how legitimate your claim, chances are they will side with your boss. His track record is proven; yours is not.

3. If you think your boss is holding back on an issue like a raise, promotion, or vacation time because the two of you don't get along, go to a neutral third party—a company ombudsman or your personnel department or even someone on his level with whom you do get along—to ask for advice. Although that person may not be able to change the situation, he may be able to bring it to the attention of someone who can. The danger of trying to argue your case with your boss's boss is that unless that person is familiar with your performance, he or she has no alternative but to rely on your boss's estimation of the situation.

You have to be prepared for repercussions from your boss, even if they're not major ones—no boss appreciates having his judgment questioned by an underling.

Getting Along with the Top Boss Better Than with Your Immediate Supervisor

Developing good rapport with the most important person in your organization has many benefits, but it can be a real liability if your immediate boss doesn't get along with him or resents the fact that you have a better relationship than he has. Even if you don't flaunt your favor, your boss may be vindictive or try to assert himself by pushing you around.

Leslie Thompson Williams's boss tried to make her look bad by reporting mistakes she made to the sales manager, with whom she got along very well. When the manager called her in for an explanation, Leslie told him that her boss had not mentioned the problems to her. Her boss continued to bad-mouth her until she blew up at him in front of his boss and asked him point-blank why he didn't confront her with them first. Even though she was right, the sales manager couldn't intercede because he didn't want to interfere with the supervisor's job, since he was otherwise a good employee.

If you're caught in a similar bind, it's best to try to minimize the friction. Keep your relationship with the head honcho low-key so that your own boss won't feel threatened. Like Leslie, you'll simply have to put up with some of the aggravation. If you show your immediate boss that your first loyalty is to him (even though you don't like or respect him as much as you do his superior), your working relationship will be much smoother.

A Good Relationship with Your Boss: How to Develop One

When I started my first job, it never occurred to me that I would have to work as hard at developing a good relationship with my boss as I would at doing the things I had been hired to do. For a lot of people, the first is actually more difficult than the second, since many first jobs are made of menial tasks. Here are some ground rules to keep in mind and to start to implement on Day One of your job:

1. *Make sure you understand your boss's expectations and priorities.* Some bosses are very clear about what they expect of you. The more disorganized your boss is, however, the less likely you will be to know what to do. So you'll have to ask. Writing down your responsibilities will help you get through your first few weeks on the job. Priorities aren't quite so easy to get a grip on; your boss may be able to tell you that getting out the weekly report supersedes any day-to-day activity, but there are always exceptions. When in doubt, ask.

2. *Keep your boss up-to-date on what you're doing.* If progress reports aren't formal office procedure, you'll have to keep your boss posted. Letting your boss know where things stand serves two purposes: it can keep a boss who bugs you too often off your back, and it reassures any boss that you're worth your paycheck.

3. *Follow up on all your boss's requests right away.* It's one of the quickest ways to gain his confidence. If you run into problems taking care of a request, let your boss know that you're trying (and, if necessary, what the holdup is) so that he'll know you're on top of the situation. Once you take care of the request, let your boss know. It's especially important in the beginning to establish credibility, to let him see that you can handle the assignments he gives you.

4. *Be willing to take on new responsibilities, even if they involve drudgery.* If you do, your boss will be more likely to consider you when a more challenging assignment comes up. And keep in mind that the most successful people usually start out at the bottom of their profession and learn the field inside out; they are able to grasp how all the small, seemingly unimportant tasks fit together and contribute to getting the job done.

5. *Try to anticipate busy times.* At the least it will take several months, and in many businesses a year, to get a feel for the rhythm of your work cycle. When you can, take advantage of calm-before-the-storm periods; if you don't know what kind of preparations can be made before the onslaught, ask your boss. He'll be impressed that you're looking ahead—it's a sign of "executive thinking." It's a good way, too, of freeing yourself for more important activities during hectic times.

6. *Don't take things your boss does—or doesn't do—too personally.* It's unrealistic to think that your boss will find it necessary to let you know about every decision he's made, every outcome of a project, every meeting that's been scheduled. Ordinary absentminded lack of communication is probably not worth mentioning. It may be, however, if you feel so out of touch with your boss's activities that you fear your work is being affected. Broach the subject by asking your boss if he would mind keeping you more closely posted on the things that you feel would make a difference—and explain how.

Women Bosses: Advice for Men

Women represent less than 5 percent of senior corporate executives, but they are well entrenched in middle-management positions.

Women bosses used to be typed one of five ways: the Queen Bee, who doesn't go out of her way to help other women move up because she enjoys her special status; the Sexy Lady, who relies on her sexuality in communicating and dealing with her colleagues; the Mother Figure, who treats those under her as if they were her children; One of the Guys, who puts aside her femininity to gain male acceptance; and the Bitch, who asserts her authority by acting tough or insensitive.

Certainly there are women bosses who fit these descriptions, but noticeably absent is a positive stereotype—a kind of female Coach, the woman boss who is understanding but firm, invites input but makes the final decision, is personable without violating her professionalism. She, too, exists and will become a more common female boss type as working for a woman becomes less the exception.

Since you're probably accustomed to working and competing with women in school, you will have fewer problems than older men do dealing with women as bosses. Still, there are always times, particularly in a first job, when a man isn't quite sure about how to relate to a female boss.

If your boss is significantly older than you are, her professional status will make it easier to take orders from her. But if your boss isn't much older than you are, occasionally you may feel like questioning her judgment or dealing with her in sexual terms. It's in your best interests to resist both urges. There probably is no faster route to a boss's blacklist than to act as if you know more than she does. And while sexual tension is almost inevitable in any male-female interaction, there is a distinct difference between harmless flirting and sexual overtures. Most female bosses vehemently resent the latter.

Giving a performance review can be particularly difficult for a female boss and a male employee. Even though women bosses say men take criticism less personally than women do, some female bosses, because they've been taught to protect men's ego, still have a hard time pointing out a male subordinate's weak points. Some women bosses try to overcome these hang-ups by delivering what sounds like hard-nosed criticism; in fact, they're only trying to distance themselves emotionally from what they're saying. Don't overestimate their emotionality, though. Most female bosses agree that it's a mistake to try to play on their emotions when you ask for a raise or special consideration.

A University of Southern California survey reports that male subordinates and women bosses have fewer problems than they anticipate. But some do arise when a women is promoted over her head. A woman in her first managerial job who lacks confidence or who isn't supported by management may have difficulty delegating responsibilities or her department may have been stripped of important work. If you work for such a boss, give the situation time to work out. She may simply need a few weeks to rise to the level her position demands; if, however, several months have gone by and nothing seems to have changed, you may want to consider transferring or even looking around for a new job. If your boss is being held back because of her inadequacies or management's chauvinism, you won't get anywhere either.

Socializing with Your Boss: The Unwritten Rules

Your boss asks you to lunch or to play tennis or to have a drink after work. What should you talk about? What are his intentions? What should you say if he brings up his problems? Will you get flak from your coworkers?

Socializing with your boss is often a tricky proposition; it can cement your professional relationship, or it can backfire and place your job, and sometimes your career, in jeopardy. To make it work, you have to keep things in perspective — even if your boss doesn't. That's hard enough when you've had several years of experience and a number of bosses, but, when you're in your first job, it can be especially difficult.

Here are some guidelines that should make out-of-the-office contacts work to your advantage.

1. *Let your boss initiate most nonworking-hours get-togethers.* The inviter is on the offensive, and it's better not to upset the balance of power, even in a social situation. The one exception is athletic interests you share. Ask him casually whether he might want to play before you suggest a specific date for a squash game.

If your boss takes the initiative and you're of the same sex, it's to your advantage to accept; if you can't make it, let him know you would be happy to some other time. If your boss is a member of the opposite sex, think twice about after-hours socializing unless he makes it clear that he wants to discuss business or it's an invitation that includes spouses or dates.

2. *Take conversational cues from your boss.* Sticking to innocuous subjects is a good idea. If your boss starts talking about his problems — in or out of the office — listen sympathetically, but don't get involved as adviser, even if he asks what you think: it disrupts the employer-employee relationship. *He's* supposed to be the authority figure — not you — even if you are close in age. Regardless of how much your boss reveals to you about himself, be sparing in what you tell him about your own personal life. Letting him in on current or past crises won't, in most circumstances, raise his opinion of you. And don't make the biggest mistake of all — trying to get otherwise classified office information out of him.

3. *Go easy on the booze (and put on your best manners).* The most powerful people, it is said, do not drink or drink lightly at business or quasi-business functions. They know that too much alcohol loosens the tongue — a liability when you are in the company of those who have power over your future. You may say something you don't mean, spill a company secret, simply come across as someone who can't hold his liquor. If your boss wants to drink, fine; if he encourages you to drink, sip slowly. Don't make the mistake of thinking you can be drinking buddies; again, that kind of social relationship destroys the balance of power in your professional relationship.

4. *Don't flaunt your friendship with your boss.* One of the dangers in getting close to your boss is that your coworkers may react badly. If you're a woman and he's a man, men on your level will resent what they perceive as your unfair sexual advantage, even if your personal relationship is platonic. Even if you and your boss are of the same gender, other members of your "team" may begin to treat you like a teacher's pet if they don't enjoy the same camaraderie. The best policy is to be tight-

lipped about your friendship and to make any out-of-the-office arrangements in private.

If you have what Michael Maccoby, author of *The Gamesman,* calls a "jungle fighter" boss (someone who has a list of enemies in the corporate world as well as a list of friends), you may find yourself in difficulty because of your friendship. Scott Jenkins was brought into the diamond-selling business by a family friend who was several years his senior. The two men got very chummy; they even vacationed together. Scott made terrific progress at his company until his boss left for a better job. Scott's new boss had not gotten along well with his former one, and he did his best to get Scott fired.

5. *Avoid sexual or romantic come-ons from your boss.* The main problem with an office romance is that it can backfire—and because you're the subordinate, you're going to end up the loser. Few people have made it up the career ladder in a horizontal position. Even if you're honestly attracted to your boss, the issue you must come to terms with is: What happens at work when your after-hours relationship falls on hard times? No matter how much your boss values you as an employee, if he feels uncomfortable, you can expect, at the very least, to be transferred. Probably you'll be fired or forced to resign.

6. *Keep an emotional distance in your personal relationship.* It is possible to have a cordial social relationship with a boss who is a member of your own sex without getting too involved. If your boss comes to mean more to you as a friend than as an employer, your expectations and possibly his may change, which inevitably will affect your work performance. He may begin to rely on you for things that are beyond your responsibilities, for example, and ultimately you may resent that. Personal relationships can help you get ahead on the job, but you can't be your own best friend if you're also the boss's.

Mentors: How They Can Give Your Career a Boost

- Soon after Charles Wilson became a newspaper reporter, a veteran reporter took him under his wing. He was an enormous influence in shaping Charles's writing style and helping him through the early months when many of his stories were rewritten.

- Amy Tanner was rescued from a first job in which she was unhappy by a high-ranking woman who hired Amy as her assistant and helped her get her next job as well.

- Jack Snyder decided to get his master's degree in counseling after he became friendly with the guidance counselor in the high school where he taught business. After earning it, he took over one of the functions of the counseling office—working with truants—on a half-day basis in addition to his teaching.

Having a mentor made a crucial difference in the direction and pace of those three careers. A mentor, simply put, is a career coach, someone in a professional or managerial position who takes a personal interest in your career. He is there to guide you, to correct you when you make mistakes your own boss may not point out to you, to give you inside information about your office or company, to introduce you to the right people.

But if you're smart and ambitious and lucky, won't you get just as far without a mentor? Maybe, maybe not. A survey of top executives in the *Harvard Business Review* found that two thirds had had one mentor, and one third had had two or more mentors. Mentors can help control the "lucky" variable in the success equation; they can put in a good word for you, tell you about opportunities you might not have heard about, encourage you to try things you might have thought were beyond your grasp.

And there are other benefits. Those executives who had mentors reported they found greater satisfaction in their work and earned on the average more money at a younger age than their mentorless counterparts. That may have been the result of having had someone to help smooth their rough edges, keep their professional problems in perspective, and intercede on their behalf in crisis situations.

Being a protégé has its risks, too. Your boss's enemies can become your enemies, because the two of you are considered a team. If your boss leaves, you will be vulnerable. Eric Dane's boss and mentor was one of the most powerful men in the company, and when he left he asked the firm's president to look out for Eric. But one of his boss's old enemies continually tried to sabotage Eric. When Eric reported one of the man's shady business practices, his enemy did everything in his power to discredit Eric. Since the company president was ill, he didn't play an active role in the company's affairs, and Eric's enemy got what he wanted — Eric's dismissal.

Finding a mentor is not unlike trying to meet a member of the opposite sex you'd like to get close to: timing is as crucial as personality, compatibility, and enthusiasm. In other words, you can't ask someone to be your mentor, but, if you find someone who might fit the bill, it doesn't hurt to create the circumstances for it to happen. That means seeking that person's opinion the next time you need advice on an office problem or a career move. Or asking him at an informal moment how he got started and whether there was someone who helped him out.

Who is most likely to be a mentor to you? Probably someone who is familiar with your work and can evaluate your potential — a department or division head or a person outside your company whom you've met through a professional organization or contact. A mentor often sees something of his younger self in a protégé and may have come from a similar background or gone to the same college.

Many mentor relationships are formed during the first five years of a career, a crucial time to have someone on your side. How you fare during those early few years has a big effect on how fast your career moves along. Almost 70 percent of the male executives in the *Harvard Business Review* study had a mentor during that period; most of the women executives found theirs between the sixth and tenth years of their career.

The advantages of a mentor are most readily apparent in a corporate setting where office politics are complicated. Having a guide to different levels of authority and at all the forks in your career path clearly has benefits. But even in a mom-and-pop operation, developing a mentor relationship with your boss is valuable for both guidance and developing contacts.

Traditionally, most mentors have been men, but that's changing as more women move into management jobs and are in a position to help out women in entry- and middle-level jobs. And an ambitious woman may need a mentor even more than an ambitious man. A comparison of successful women and men found that the one success factor cited in the case of all the women surveyed was "help from above"; that was the case with only 55 percent of the men. Even women not interested in making it to the top find having a mentor makes their lives easier.

Leslie Thompson Williams credits her fast-moving career to a mentor, whom Leslie met on her first job as a secretary. The mentor was the only woman and the only black on the television sales staff. She befriended Leslie, who was six years her junior, and encouraged her to go into sales because it was a field that promised freedom, money, and a great deal of contact with people. Leslie decided to transfer to a sales-trainee position.

If there isn't a role-model woman in your office who could function as your mentor, you might look for one in a professional organization. New groups are providing women with a setting for exchanging information about job problems (and solutions), employment opportunities, and professional gossip. The groups function much as the old-boy network operates for men.

Many mentor relationships grow beyond professional life; a high percentage of top executives say theirs developed into lengthy friendships. It helps to have a guardian angel in your professional life, so be on the lookout for high-ranking executives with halos.

8

Office Politics

*The Office Hierarchy: Who's Important and
Who's Not . . . Double-Talk: How to
Figure Out What People Really Mean . . .
An Engaging Personality: A Sure Way to Win
Office Allies . . . Gossip: Should You
Plug In or Tune Out? . . . Brownnosing:
A Way up the Success Ladder? . . . Enemies:
Who's Out to Get You and Why . . .
Being Your Own Best Competition*

During my first year on the job, I was under the mistaken impression that the way to get ahead was to show up regularly and do good work. What I eventually discovered was that, while those things helped, becoming an active participant in office politics gave me an enormous edge over the person who let his work speak for itself.

Office politics is an undercurrent created by the ambitions of certain staff members who are manipulating, lobbying, and jockeying for greater power and influence within the organization. Generally, the bigger the office, the more complicated the politics because of the number of personalities involved. Your success on the job very likely will be affected by office politics if you work in a field in which any assessment of your job performance is highly subjective, especially advertising, the arts, and politics. But even if you work in a field with more objective performance criteria, there's no avoiding office politics. Whether or not you enjoy the game, you will at some point find yourself caught up in it. The best way to become a savvy player is to:

- Cultivate relationships with the "right people," whose opinions or decisions can influence your career future.

- Avoid turf that is already staked out — it's much smarter to carve out your own area of expertise.

- Keep your ambitions in line with business considerations. (You can't, for example, expect your boss to agree to expanding your responsibilities to cover a new area if the company's sales are sagging.)

There are no hard-and-fast rules in office politics; each office has its own set. Use your first few months on the job to observe the subtle and not so subtle ways in which people maneuver to get the best possible deal for themselves.

The Office Hierarchy: Who's Important and Who's Not

An important puzzle to piece together is where those with whom you work fit. You can get the system down more quickly by writing down the name and job of everyone you meet. Once you understand the organizational relationship of your coworkers to your boss, the department, and the company, the tidbits of information you'll come across on a daily basis will have a lot more meaning.

Getting to know certain key people in your office or organization can make your daily work a lot easier and can help boost your career. They include:

1. *The head honcho.* He may be the head of your division, the owner, or the president of the company; he's the one with the ultimate say over you and your boss's fate. In the end, it's his opinion of you that matters most. If you've never come in contact with him in your day-to-day work, create opportunities for him to get to know you — by speaking up at meetings, making small talk, or showing up in his office from time to time, even if it's only to deliver a memo.

2. *The department manager.* If your boss isn't the head of the department, make sure that the person who is gets to know you and your work. He probably is involved in your raises and promotions, and, if your boss doesn't look out for you, this person may — if he's aware of your contributions. You can keep him posted by mentioning how projects are coming along or by mentioning a client's reaction to a job you did.

3. *The support staff.* These are the people who help process other people's work and keep the business flowing smoothly. They include secretaries, mail clerks, messengers, and copy machine operators. Too few professionals realize the value of the work support people perform, and they don't bother to get to know them personally and often treat them as if their contributions don't matter. Make it a point to learn the names of support staff, even if you deal with them only occasionally. Establishing a friendly rapport can make your work and theirs more pleasant, and they will be willing to help you out when you're in a pinch.

Many people in support jobs are important because of their relationship to people in power. Secretaries, for example, can clue you in on whether their bosses are in a bad mood, advise you on how to make a special request, or tell you what the current status of a project is. But you cannot expect to get the inside track if your interest surfaces only when you need help.

4. *The office manager.* It's smart to become buddies with him because he usually has control of small but important things — room assignments, furniture, equipment. You're more likely to get faster action or even a special request granted if you're on good terms with him.

Double-Talk: How to Figure Out What People Really Mean

People don't always mean what they say; and what they say isn't always what they mean. Double-talk is as prevalent in offices as it is in relationships — it's used to assert power, communicate dissatisfaction, and influence behavior. Some double-talk is deliberate — if a person doesn't want to hurt your feelings by being brutally honest, he couches his language indirectly and leaves the inferences up to you. Some double-talk is cowardly — if a person can't bring himself to complain or deliver bad news, he may drop hints and hope you get the message.

Types of Double-Talk

Double-talk in the office comes in many varieties, which you may have a hard time recognizing at first. The most common are:

1. *The tease.* Humor is an easy way to bring something bothersome to someone's attention. It's usually used when the matter isn't terribly serious but is worth a warning.

2. *Misplaced irritation.* Rather than telling you what's really on his mind, the double-talker zeroes in on something unrelated to the problem. His criticism or shortness may catch you off guard.

3. *The coded message.* English majors may have an edge with this kind of double-talk because it's loaded with innuendo. There's no explicitness here; you have to read between the lines. Example: At five o'clock on Friday, your boss says, "These reports should be proofread by Monday morning." Translation: He wants this done over the weekend.

4. *The cool tone of voice.* Nothing is said directly, but conversation is less friendly than usual. Often, this kind of double-talk is used when the person isn't sure how he feels about a situation or what to say about a problem.

5. *The avoidance.* Things have to be pretty serious if this tactic is used. It can mean the other person is pretty teed off and hasn't decided how to respond, or he may want you to notice and ask what's wrong.

Handling the Situation

Knowing how to translate double-talk is a skill worth developing. It's usually a matter of being sensitive to the nuances of human dynamics.

Here are a few pointers:

1. How often a double-talk situation has come up before is one indication of how to respond to it — if frequently, it usually can be ignored. If a senior staff member kids you about how little time it took you to hand in a report, for example, the comment could imply that you did a rush job, in which case it's important to reassure him that everything he asked for is there. But if he teases other coworkers, it's probably just his way of being friendly and letting you know he noticed your speed.

2. If you suspect that someone is trying to tell you something, but it's not clear what, don't always press for an explanation. The other person may feel pushed into a corner and inadvertently blurt out what he really thinks, and that may be something you don't really want to know.

3. You should try to clarify what a person means, however, if the confusion could affect your work. If, for example, your boss tells you to make sure the layouts are done properly, you may understandably wonder whether there was something wrong with the last ones you turned in. You can ask whether there's any way you can improve on the last batch. If the answer is no, you'll know that there was no "warning" intended by his remark.

An Engaging Personality: A Sure Way to Win Office Allies

Just how can an engaging personality help you on the job? It can:

- Predispose people to be receptive to your suggestions because they know that at the least you're pleasant to deal with.
- Make you a popular choice to include on team projects because your personality won't interfere with getting the job done.
- Help you get your way without seeming like a manipulator because people think of you as reasonable.
- Help you make the sale, clinch the deal, or get information because people like dealing with someone whom they like.

It's to your advantage to earn a reputation early on for being easy to get along with. You don't have to have an outgoing personality; being personable has to do more with the way you treat people.

One of the fastest ways to win friends is by being a good listener. Everyone likes to talk to someone who appears genuinely interested in what he has to say. Even if your end of the conversation is limited to asking questions or making comments, you'll make a great impression simply because you made that person feel important.

It's actually quite simple to get people on your side. Make it a point to learn your coworkers' outside interests and ask questions about them (family, pets, and hobbies are sure bets). Even the smallest gesture — a birthday card, flowers on a special occasion, a sympathy note if someone close dies — won't be forgotten. Honest compliments are another way to cultivate allies in the office. No matter what their job level, your coworkers will appreciate being told that you were impressed with something they did and being asked a few questions about it. If you're not in a position to do that very often, complimenting someone on his appearance is a way of breaking the ice and building the groundwork for a pleasant working relationship.

Whenever the opposite sex is involved, there is a fine line between being friendly and coming on. Flirting — even if it's done in an apparently harmless, teasing way — or overly casual body language — sitting on someone's desk or standing too close — is likely to be misinterpreted. You stand a much better chance of earning your coworkers' respect and support if you deal with them in a pleasant but professional way.

Gossip: Should You Plug In or Tune Out?

The bigger the company you work for, the more active the office grapevine will be. Rumors, hearsay, and speculation are common when there are many layers in the formal channels of communication.

There are two basic types of gossip that dominate office grapevines: people talk (the variety that involves people's social and sex lives) and business banter (who's getting hired, fired, or promoted and what's being said behind management's closed doors).

Generally, it's smart to avoid people gossip — it's not important to your job, and whispering with coworkers in the halls doesn't look professional. Business banter, on the other hand, can clue you in on how your coworkers feel about their jobs and the company, things they're not likely to reveal in the course of conducting normal business. You also may come across information helpful to getting ahead.

The trick to using gossip wisely is to be a passive participant: to listen but not repeat what you hear. It's easy for new employees to self-destruct by misinterpreting information or passing along the wrong information to the wrong people. Your coworkers will be much more willing to let you in on things if they know the gossip doesn't go any farther than you. Try to limit your comments to, "That's interesting." If sources expect you to let them in on juicy tidbits you come across, you can either plead lack of access or pass on innocuous information.

Before you decide to make a move on the basis of gossip you've heard, check it out further. Most gossip is like a hot tip on the stock market; 90 percent of the time you'll lose money. The first checkpoint is the reliability of your source — if you haven't been around long enough to know that his information is usually on target, you'll be taking an enormous risk. If you can, try to determine whether the rumor originated with someone who really is in the know or would have access to the information. One way to verify the information is to question other people whose opinions you respect by simply asking, "Have you heard anything about . . .?" without passing along details.

Rumors concerning changes or things about to happen in an office sometimes are instigated deliberately by management to test-market people's responses or to prepare them for bad news. That kind of rumor is worth checking out, particularly if it will have an impact on your job if true. If the matter is serious enough, you may want to ask your boss, who is more likely to have an answer than your coworkers. If the kind of rumor it is makes that sticky, ask an experienced member of the staff for his reading.

Soliciting legitimate information is not quite the same as gossiping. If you're eager to find out what your boss thought about your ideas for a departmental project, there's nothing wrong with asking a senior staff member to tell you what he's heard.

Brownnosing: A Way up the Success Ladder?

Brownnosers are easy to spot: they're the ones who laugh at the boss's stupid jokes, pay him undeserved compliments, and hang breathless in his most boring ruminations. The question is: Does that help them get ahead? It does — sometimes. Insecure people in powerful positions need to be reassured that their ideas are good and that they are important, and they often surround themselves with people who will supply that support.

You may be able to land a new job or better assignments by currying favor with a superior, but your colleagues will see your behavior for what it is and like you less for it. Isolating yourself from your peers may have no immediate effect on your career, but in five or ten years, when they're moving into positions of influence, that may make a difference.

The second "cost" of being a brownnoser is losing your self-respect. Some people are able to rationalize their behavior by telling themselves it's all in pursuit of a greater good. Others think of it as a game and feel they're playing their bosses for fools. But somewhere down the line, every thinking person asks himself: Am I stooping too low simply to get ahead?

Jayne Krissen accepted the invitation to lunch of a senior project director whose reputation was mud among her coworkers: He played them against one another. Jayne was flattered by his interest in her and said nothing when he made derisive comments about her coworkers. She decided it was worth putting up with him to get better assignments. He finally took away a prize assignment from a colleague (and good friend of hers) with whom he was unjustly displeased and offered it to Jayne. She realized that, if she accepted it, she would compromise something that was more important to her. She declined it, claiming she had too many other pressing projects. From that point on, her relationship with the project director cooled off, but she felt comfortable with her decision.

Even if you've never engaged in obsequious behavior before, you may be tempted to use a few brownnosing techniques to promote a good relationship with your boss or with others you want to impress. Bosses are susceptible to flattery; you can try it, but if you aren't able, as writer Harry Stein put it, "to curry favor so deftly that it passes for simple courtesy or tact or insight or charm," your brownnosing may backfire, and your motives may always be suspect. It's better to project an eager-to-please and supportive attitude and work for the kind of employee-boss relationship in which there is room for intelligent differences of opinion, a quality any enlightened boss will appreciate.

Enemies: Who's Out to Get You and Why

Knowing who your enemies are is as important as knowing your friends. The most dangerous enemies are people with clout—even if your work is satisfactory, they can undermine your career, simply because their opinions matter. You may have made an enemy of someone because you did something inadvertently that was detrimental to him. You may be a target because you're bright and he's insecure. Or you may never know why he dislikes you.

My first bona fide enemy appeared on the scene during my first year on the job. I was assigned to edit a column she had been editing because the managing editor wasn't pleased with her work. I didn't realize the extent of her resentment until several months later when she delayed editing a piece I had written. Nothing I said could persuade her to move on it. Finally, I took the risk of mentioning it to our mutual boss. The piece was edited, but my last-resort move didn't improve our relationship. Fortunately, she wasn't an office "heavy."

The three most common types of enemies lurking in the work world are idea or credit stealers, backstabbers, and male or age chauvinists. Here's how they operate and what you can do to counter their actions.

Idea or Credit Stealers

"Ideas are power because ideas are money," wrote Jane Trahey, one of the most successful women in advertising. There are plenty of ideas floating around, but few of them are good and workable. Learning how to protect and get credit for strokes of genius is as important as coming up with them. That's especially true if you work in a creative field, where you're only as promotable as your ideas are good.

Initially, you'll have to send up a lot of trial balloons to make sure your ideas are on the right track. When your boss finally says, "Let's give it a try," you may not be the person responsible for implementing it unless it's a very small idea. And the person who can make an idea work usually gets more kudos than the person who suggested it. Nevertheless, don't hesitate to claim your share of credit. And if someone takes what's yours, protest. It's not uncommon for people to start thinking of something as theirs simply because they offered a few details. The best way to guard against theft of credit is to stay in control of an idea. Unless your boss is willing to trust you entirely with implementing it, at least stay in contact with the person who is.

Occasionally, there is out-and-out thievery. The best ways to protect your ideas and make sure you get the credit for your work are:

1. *Put your suggestion in writing.* Even if that's not required, it's a good idea to boil an idea down to the barest essentials and explain how it might be accomplished. A written suggestion shows that you've given the idea some thought and that you're serious about it. In addition to that, it's the best protection against someone's claiming later that the idea was his.

2. *Bring up your suggestion at the right time and place.* Save your best ideas (or the ones you would like to work on yourself) for individual discussion with your boss rather than bringing them up in a meeting, where they're more likely to be altered, lost in the shuffle, or taken away from you. If doing that is out of line in your office, distinguish a pet idea from one you're "handing out" by saying you would be willing to take responsibility for it if it's approved.

3. *Talk to the credit grabber before he makes the steal official.* If you notice that your name isn't on the memo to which you contributed significant thoughts or that someone is about to kidnap your brainchild, don't hesitate to call him on it. Say that you were surprised to see his name attached or your name omitted; the grabber may back down immediately or say that it was an oversight. If he insists on holding your idea captive, you'll have to decide whether it makes more sense to mention it to your boss and make an issue of it, or forget it this time and be more wary in the future.

Backstabbers

They can be the biggest threat only because you may not learn of their undermining for months. Their motive: jealousy. Their tactic: spreading lies about you and misrepresenting your work. Once you discover a backstabber (a friend will probably clue you in), your best course of action depends on how great the damage is and on how much weight your enemy packs. You may want to ignore him; you may want to try to talk out your differences and reach some kind of truce. If matters are serious, you may have to talk to your boss; reassure him that you're putting in your best effort or that rumors that have been circulating about you simply aren't true. Don't be accusatory; just set the record straight. Reciprocal backstabbing probably will only aggravate the situation and can give the backstabber more ammunition if you're not as good at being underhanded as he is.

People who chronically undermine the efforts of others in order to make themselves look good eventually lose their credibility. So, if everything else fails, you may win in the end by simply riding out the bad times and outlasting your enemy.

Male or Age Chauvinists

The reason they put you down is that they're threatened by you. Drawing battle lines by telling them what you think of their behavior will usually only worsen the situation. But if you ignore them, you may lose out on assignments or opportunities.

Chauvinists can be won over because their gripe with you isn't personal; it's against age or sex. One way to respond is with humor, though if they read poking fun at the situation as taking a dig at them, they'll only be alienated further. Another tactic is to ask their advice; you don't have to take it—the point is to give them an opening to get to know and trust you. If neither of these approaches works, you might try dealing with them head on. Point out that despite any personal differences you may have you would like to establish a good working relationship. If you take a dispassionate, professional stance, the chauvinist may go along as a matter of pride.

Being Your Own Best Competition

If you went to an academically rigorous college, you're used to competitiveness among your peers. If you didn't, you may feel taken aback when you notice all your office colleagues looking out for Number One.

It's natural to compare yourself with your peers, but rating your own career progress against theirs is difficult. Careers move ahead at different speeds, and how fast you move up has as much to do with business considerations (how quickly your department is growing or how soon someone leaves the job you aspire to) as it does with your job performance. You can be your own best competition if you follow these suggestions:

1. *Don't talk openly about your ambitions.* If your short-term aspirations happen to be the same as those of the person you tell, you've just created the makings of an all-out competition. The only person in the office worth telling (at the appropriate time) is your boss or another person making decisions that can affect you.

2. *Base your decisions about short- and long-term goals on your needs, not your colleagues' plans.* You can get sidetracked if you are influenced by peer opinions about which assignments or moves are desirable.

3. *If your office is openly competitive, don't be a wallflower.* If you're not comfortable being openly aggressive, promote your work rather than yourself.

4. *Get to know your strengths and weaknesses by trying a variety of tasks.* Limit serious competition to those areas in which you excel. If there's an assignment or project up for grabs, figure out what parts of it you're particularly qualified to do and use that as a basis for selling your boss on assigning it to you.

If someone who's junior to you is given an assignment or promotion that took you longer to earn, there's nothing to be gained from a sour-grapes attitude. Malcolm McDonnell worked in his sales job for a year before he was given his own list of customers. When a coworker got his list after only seven months on the job, Malcolm complained to his boss. His boss's reaction was anger — the company had expanded its business more quickly than anticipated, another salesman was needed, and Malcolm's coworker was next in line. You're usually not in a position to judge the reason for a management decision, and you can really stick your foot in your mouth if you criticize it.

You also may have to deal with being the less experienced (and resented) person. Several months into her first job as a news assistant at a TV station, Erlene Berry Wilson noticed a lot of tension between her and her immediate supervisor, the assignment editor. Erlene was making an effort to learn everything she could about her boss's job because she figured that would equip her for a reporter's job. But the station was undergoing a staff reorganization, and Erlene's boss felt threatened by her initiative. Erlene reassured him that she wasn't trying to move into his territory. It worked; in fact, he eventually suggested that she fill in for him when he was on vacation.

The best course of action to take if your boss seems threatened by you is to keep him informed of what you're doing. If he still feels threatened and begins to tighten his control over your job and generally makes life miserable for you, you'll have to choose between saying something, waiting it out, or leaving. The only time it makes sense to talk to your boss's superior is when you know your own boss is probably on his way out the door.

9

Coworkers

*Popularity and Respect: How Important
Are They? . . . Status: Knowing Where You Fit
In . . . Office Cliques: Should You Get Involved
or Avoid Them? . . . The Team Mentality: How
to Become an Accepted Team Player . . .
The Most Common Problems: How to Handle
Them . . . Dating Colleagues: When It's
Likely to Jeopardize Your Job*

They may become friends, lovers, enemies, roommates, or simply acquaintances with whom you spend 8 hours a day. Coworkers can make your work more enjoyable, give you headaches that aspirin won't relieve, help you move up, or cause you to cash in your chips at a company prematurely.

Developing good working relationships with your colleagues won't happen overnight. Your colleagues have to get used to having you around, spend time getting to know you, and find out what you're capable of and willing to do. In some companies, you won't really belong unless you share in some of the after-work activities of your colleagues.

The pointers below contain the collective wisdom of successful people whose working relationships have ranged from disastrous to made-in-heaven.

1. *Stay away from losers.* They often latch on to unsuspecting newcomers since everyone else has their number. No matter how on the ball you are, you will lose out big being linked with a loser.

2. *Be a regular Joe.* Don't express the full range of your idiosyncrasies — save the rarer treasures for your friends and family.

3. *Don't reveal too much about yourself.* Until you figure out who's on your side, keep a low profile. You don't know how what you say may be interpreted or whether it might be used against you.

4. *Make friendly overtures.* Most people won't go out of their way to befriend you; you'll have to take an interest in them before they will extend invitations to you.

5. *Find a sponsor.* The best way to learn the ropes is to buddy up with someone who has been there for six months to a year. His advice on whom to avoid, what to expect, and office protocol can be helpful. But keep in mind that that is only one person's perspective.

6. *Don't bad-mouth your coworkers.* Even if you can't stand the person with whom you share a cubicle, don't spread your complaints around to seemingly sympathetic ears. Having your differences broadcast to others will do you no good.

7. *Don't take it personally if someone doesn't like you.* Even if you were president of your fraternity or homecoming queen, there will be people who will dislike the way you look, walk, talk, or dress. Act friendly anyway—you have nothing to lose.

8. *Pattern yourself after the office hotshot.* Don't be obvious about it, but work at incorporating some of his better qualities and ways of operating into your routine. They're bound to improve your performance.

9. *Try to resolve differences on your own.* Bosses don't like to get involved in personal feuds, even if they do involve office matters.

Popularity and Respect: How Important Are They?

Being popular, at least among your own friends, may have been important to you in college. But the qualities that made you popular in college are not necessarily those that score points in the office, at least among people who count. It's much less important for you to be well liked by your peers than to be highly regarded by your boss and his peers.

Ann Tucker had no problem making friends when she started her first job; she was a natural "ham" and enjoyed entertaining people with her stories. Her boss and other managers enjoyed her sense of humor, too, but her playfulness kept them from taking her seriously. It took Ann several years to realize that being the recipient of the "Miss Congeniality" award in her office was holding her back from moving up.

There's a lot to be said for being well liked. In addition to the ego satisfaction it brings, being popular can help you land better assignments and even help you get promoted. Talented people with abrasive personalities do get promoted, but good people who are also pleasant to be around certainly have an edge.

The personality traits that are more likely to get high ratings from the people whose opinions matter are being enthusiastic about your job, offering to help out other people, and acting friendly but low-key. You don't have to repress your personality if you're outgoing, but if you're too rah-rah you'll be pegged as a cheerleader.

Small gestures are more likely to earn you popularity points at first than are grandiose ones — for example, lending a sympathetic ear when a coworker has a problem, expressing your appreciation when someone goes out of his way for you, and doing small favors will make you an office favorite.

Even more important than being popular on the job is being respected. Your work style is sometimes more important than your job performance — your coworkers' opinions will be based on how you deal with them in getting results. It's important not to underestimate the influence coworkers, especially office "stars," have on your career. Your boss's impressions — good or bad — are likely to be reinforced by the feedback he gets from your colleagues.

One of the surest routes to earning respect is using discretion. Quite simply, that means knowing when to keep your mouth shut. It's very tempting to flaunt the importance of your job or establish friendships by mentioning a tidbit of information you know because of your position. But in the long run, you'll be much more respected by your boss and your coworkers if they know that you can be trusted to keep confidential information to yourself.

Status: Knowing Where You Fit In

I was working for several weeks before I realized that in the eyes of the other ten people in my department I was, in a nutshell, a peon. I happened to be an important peon because I was the assistant to the head of the department. But that distinction notwithstanding, I nonetheless held the least prestigious job. If that's your lot, it doesn't matter where you went to school, what your grade point average was, or where you've worked before.

It's important to know what your job status is because it should affect how you deal with your coworkers. The word *coworkers* is misleading — it implies equality; in fact, there is no such thing as equality among employees. You may have the same job title and even similar responsibilities, but that doesn't make you equal. Other factors determine status: how long you've been there, who your boss is (the more important he is, the higher your rank), and your unofficial rank — the esteem in which you're held by your boss and your colleagues whose opinions matter.

Your status is especially hard to determine if your initial job is somewhat above normal entry level. If they resent you — and they may — your coworkers will be quick to pick up on your weaknesses and mistakes and slow to help you out. The best way to win them over is to avoid flaunting your position and to show your respect for experience by asking for advice. People who are in positions much higher than yours are less likely to be threatened by you; you can and should sound self-confident about what you're doing when you're dealing with them; that makes you seem competent.

An important status distinction is between line and staff jobs. People in line jobs are directly responsible for producing your company's product or service. People in staff jobs provide services to people in line jobs. Personnel, publicity, payroll, accounting, advertising, and travel departments typically provide support services. Often people in line jobs have a don't-bother-me attitude toward people in staff jobs or don't understand how staff work helps them. Gail Kislevitz made that discovery during her first few months as a personnel assistant with a bank. Her assignment was to find out the job responsibilities of people in different bank divisions so that her department could keep job descriptions up-to-date. She found out through trial and error that the best way to get people to cooperate was to explain who specifically was requesting the information and what it was going to be used for.

Another "rank" distinction that takes time—and a few experiences—to resolve is determining which coworkers have authority over you. Even if you work directly for one boss, there will no doubt be times when a coworker asks you to do something for him. Suppose you're not particularly busy, and the task you're asked to do isn't particularly interesting. Do you refuse, try to get out of it, or say, "No problem"? If the person is a department "heavy," it's usually wise to cooperate cheerfully. If that's not the case, and you suspect your coworker is trying to get out of a job himself, mention it to your boss to see how he reacts. If he says, "That's Jack's job," you'll be off the hook; if not, you'll know where you stand.

A tricky status situation to handle is that of a woman asked by a male coworker to type or run an errand for him. If he's on your job level (even if he has been there longer), you don't want to set a precedent. Let him know, politely but firmly, that that's not your job. If, on the other hand, the coworker's position is higher than yours, you'll have to size up the situation. If he's in a pinch and you don't mind cultivating his good will, it's probably worth cooperating. But if you stand to gain anything, explain diplomatically how you feel about doing "favors"—it will only be harder to refuse the next time.

One of the worst "sins" you can commit when you're in a first job is to pull rank. The adage that the shortest distance between two points is a straight line doesn't work in an office hierarchy. In her first job as a researcher for a polling organization, Karen Lotte decided to call a department manager for information rather than one of the people working under him. She got it, but her boss received three complaints from the people she had bypassed. What Karen didn't understand is that organizational structures often function on ego rather than efficiency. It's important to make people feel needed, which may mean going to the lowest-level person first. You may think you're streamlining your work by going directly to a source, but the high-ranking person may be put off that an underling (you) had the nerve to call him.

Office Cliques: Should You Get Involved or Avoid Them?

Starting a full-time, permanent job can be lonely; unlike college or graduate school, there usually isn't a group of people sharing the same new experiences with you. You will be an outsider. Should you try to get in?

Office cliques are informal group structures, but they are important in some offices because they give their members a sense of belonging. There are three common types of office cliques:

1. *The social clique.* Primarily a group of employees (often in nonprofessional jobs) who are friends in and outside the office. They're usually more concerned with keeping up with each other's private lives than with discussing business.

2. *The business clique.* Their big interest is keeping up with office and industry goings-on. They may lunch, have drinks, or play sports together often, but purely social get-togethers are infrequent.

3. *The newcomers' clique.* This group is usually more flexible than the other two: the members' common bond is their lack of experience; their primary function is to provide moral support for each other. In big cities, newcomers' cliques are likely to function in both social and work settings since many entry-level employees know few other people in town.

When you're new in an office, it's smart to simply observe who is friendly with whom, and how any one group of employees is regarded by the rest of the office. If your first job is a low-level one that you plan to use as a stepping-stone, you may sell yourself short if you link up with a group of your peers who don't share your aspirations. Better to cultivate the friendship of people whose jobs you eventually would like to move into.

In some offices, the nature of the work lends itself to the formation of business cliques, and, if you work closely with a group on the job, you will be included almost automatically in after-hours activities. In her first job as a news assistant, Erlene Berry Wilson was often on the job until 7:30 at night, at which point the reporters and directors regularly went out for drinks or dinner. Getting together informally was a good way to wind down and talk about the technicalities and problems of the show they had just finished. Erlene learned things that would have taken much longer to pick up on the job.

If you're the only woman or one of few on your level, it may be hard to break into an all-male office clique. When Phyllis Chasen began working in the sports division of a manufacturing company, the one other woman in her office wasn't included in her male coworkers' after-work drinks. Phyllis realized that if she wanted to be asked along, she would have to make an extra effort to befriend the men. She never regretted taking the time because her tact worked. Becoming a member of the

117

group made her privy to information she never would have had otherwise.

The Team Mentality: How to Become an Accepted Team Player

In college you no doubt worked on your own most of the time and were graded on your individual efforts. In the working world, few things are not a group endeavor, and generally it's the success of the project that counts.

A team effort can mean working with ten other people or just one. It may be highly structured with meetings, progress reports, and delegated assignments. Or it may be so loosely structured, you're scarcely aware it is a team project.

As a rookie, you won't often be told how your assignment fits or even what the project is. There's usually no harm in asking what you're working on, but it's not wise to press the issue if your boss or the project leader is reluctant to answer.

If you're the team's junior member, you will almost certainly be given a job no one else wants. It's important to learn the rules — both spoken and unspoken — by which teams in your company play: for instance, whether team members can contribute ideas that don't deal directly with their own assignment, or whether problems that come up are solved by the team as a whole.

Here are some of the traps rookies fall into when they're working on a team project:

1. *Overstepping the bounds of your responsibility.* It's one thing to take the initiative with your task, but you should be wary about trying to prove your competence at something that's being tended to by more experienced team members. Suppose you are the newest law associate in your office, for example, and your assignment is to check the citations in a brief that's been written by several lawyers senior to you. In the course of your research, you come across a case no one has cited that might strengthen the argument. Your team's interest — and your own — can benefit more if you tell your immediate superior about your finding rather than write a memo on the case to impress him and the rest of the team.

2. *Working in too much isolation.* Suppose you are compiling test-market data for the marketing department of a consumer products division. Two weeks into your research, you check back with the team leader, only to find that the test market was changed but no one bothered telling you. Not only did you lose a week of work, but you're now a week behind schedule. By keeping in informal touch you'll eliminate the chance of wrong turns and duplications.

3. *Getting bogged down in details.* As a researcher for a television talk show, your assignment is to prepare material for an upcoming segment

on the sex life of polar bears. Before you realize it, the deadline is here, and you haven't even begun to organize the reams of material you've collected. Being thorough may be a virtue in academia, but being thorough at the expense of being on time is not acceptable in the working world. If time is running out and you're behind, ask the project leader or your boss for advice.

4. *Feeling you're done once you've completed your assigned responsibility.* If your work didn't take as long as anticipated, ask the team leader if there's anything else you can do. If you see a loose end that needs tying, take the initiative and tie it.

5. *Putting in less than your best effort because your role is unimportant.* Your brokerage house is doing a massive study of the computer industry, and you're assigned to assemble the annual reports of 300 companies. Because the task is routine, you don't notice that the report of a fast-growing foreign company is missing. The omission isn't discovered until late into the senior analysts' work. A mistake or holdup that is caused by your carelessness will be held against you, which is why you should spend time and energy to do a job right.

6. *Boasting about your work outside the company.* You're working as a junior copywriter on a team that is designing an ad campaign in the hopes of winning an account for which several agencies are competing. You casually mention to an acquaintance the hot new brainstorm your group just came up with and ask him to keep it secret. Information whispered in just those circumstances has a way of falling into the wrong hands. There's no guarantee that the leak won't be traced back to you, and similar-type innocent remarks have occasionally cost people their jobs.

You'll have to contend with a motley crew of personalities on team projects — freeloaders, procrastinators, ringleaders, and worrywarts. The trick to getting along is to remain levelheaded under pressure, stay clear of people's egos, and couch your disagreements in terms of the project's best interest. It's a good idea to keep your ego in the closet as a rookie, but that doesn't mean you have to tolerate abuse from egomaniacs. Joe Tabacco was assigned to work on a project with a more experienced lawyer who was considered "difficult." They spent a week and a half traveling together, interviewing prospective witnesses for a case. When Joe made a slight tactical mistake, his colleague accused him of incompetence and berated him in front of a witness. Joe suggested they discuss the matter later. He was so angry and humiliated that he felt like taking a swing at his colleague. After cooling off, Joe admitted that he had been wrong but said he didn't think the mistake warranted such a severe reaction. The lawyer was so taken aback by Joe's evenhandedness that he apologized for his behavior — and they had no similar problems working together after that.

The point is: if you know how to keep your cool, smooth ruffled feathers, and project a professional "Don't tread on me" image, you'll probably earn the cooperation of even the most impossible coworker.

The Most Common Problems: How to Handle Them

How well you get along with your coworkers may affect your future with the company. That doesn't mean you have to like everyone or bend over backward to please. It does mean that you should be able to handle problem personalities and deal with differences of opinion without involving the rest of the office or your boss.

Here are some of the most common coworker problems:

1. *Obnoxious habits.* The smaller your office, the bigger a problem your coworkers' habits can be. Gum-chewers, knuckle-crackers, and loud talkers or laughers can drive you to distraction, at least on days when nothing is going right. If your officemate's eccentric behavior doesn't disrupt your own work or isn't something that can easily be changed, it's usually best to grin and bear it. If his habit really does interfere with your concentration and you can't solve the problem by rearranging the work space, mention it. Explain what's bothering you and why, and if possible suggest a solution. Your coworker may not even have realized that his behavior bothered you. If that doesn't work, tell the office manager or your boss that you'd appreciate switching your work area when space becomes available.

2. *Invasions of privacy.* The best way to keep private matters quiet is to eliminate their intrusion during office hours. Tell your friends that you prefer to be called at home. Make what calls you must during the lunch hour, when most people are away, or use a pay phone. Office busybodies generally can be put off without creating bad feelings by turning their questions aside with a joke or giving a general but noncommittal answer.

3. *Incompetence that affects your work.* When your own job performance is at stake—if, say, you have to wait for your coworker to give you his work before you can start doing your own—don't hesitate to act tough. If his work is delayed or not done satisfactorily, express your dissatisfaction in no uncertain terms. Let him know that it's his responsibility to do it right if he hasn't or to notify your mutual boss if he's late, so that an adjustment can be made. If his foul-up nonetheless affects your work, explain to your boss the conditions under which you had to complete the work. Don't attack your coworker; just lay out the facts and let your boss draw his own conclusions. If you don't let him know, you may be the one whose work is criticized.

4. *Personality conflicts.* Sooner or later, you'll have to work with someone you can't stand. Unfortunately, you can't afford to let bad chemistry stand in the way of your working relationship. Early in my career, I got saddled with working with a woman who lacked polish, talked too

much, and was in general a nerd. I did nothing to cultivate her goodwill, even though that was crucial to our joint projects. Finally I realized that life would be easier if I made an effort to develop a friendly working relationship. I inquired pleasantly about the health of her dog and her two children and got on with business.

One last hint: letting others know how you really feel about someone is not a smart move. Even if they're not bosom buddies, your remarks can get back. And that may destroy forever the possibility of getting along, even professionally.

Dating Colleagues: When It's Likely to Jeopardize Your Job

Water-cooler flirting is a fact of life at most companies, but a full-fledged romance can harm your career.

No matter how discreet you are, it's virtually impossible to keep office liaisons a secret. Your coworkers have too intimate a knowledge of your comings and goings, phone calls, and office visitors not to recognize a romantic relationship. Here are dating situations to avoid at all costs (unless you're convinced the other person is the love of your life) and ones to approach with caution.

To Avoid

1. *Someone in the power structure.* There's no way that your work ever finds its way to his desk, so what difference does it make if the two of you want to get together outside of working hours? Plenty. In this case, it's other people's reactions that can put you in a compromising position. Ashley Carlton worked in a government agency and began dating a high-ranking official on the staff. They kept their secret for a while, but then they ran into a colleague at a weekend resort. When that happened, Ashley noticed a change; her boyfriend's colleagues told her things hoping she would influence him or at least pass along the information. She realized before long she had a lot to lose and little to gain by being a pawn in a game of office politics, and she ended the affair.

2. *Someone who works in your department.* Even if you're on the same job level, a romantic relationship poses several problems. If one of you becomes disenchanted, the atmosphere will be strained. If things work out, you'll be distracted, whether that's because you're madly in love or having a fight. If you decide to get married, one of you will have to transfer or resign if that's your company's policy. The person who leaves is usually the woman.

3. *Someone whose work you supervise.* This is the flip side of the socializing-with-your-boss dilemma. As a retail store sales supervisor, Bob Allen worked with many eligible young women he was interested in going out with. But he limited his social contact to having lunch with them in a

group since he scheduled their hours and supervised their work. He didn't want any of them to complain to his boss that he was playing favorites, and the easiest way to avoid that was not to ask any one out on a date.

Proceed with Caution

1. *Someone on your level who works in another department.* If your paths don't cross in the course of the day, you should run into no major problems. But don't count on your love life being private: offices are full of people who love monitoring office romances and keeping others posted. That can create problems for the relationship, at least in its early stages; neither does it help if you want to keep the liaison quiet.

2. *Clients.* The potential problems here are leaks of confidential information and loss of professional objectivity. Some employers, including large accounting firms, actually prohibit the practice. Even if you're smart enough to avoid business pillow talk, there may be flak. If your employer perceives a conflict of interest, you may find yourself choosing between your job and your relationship—if you're given a choice at all.

10
Ethics

Freebies: Understanding Their True Cost . . .
Petty Theft on the Job: Fringe Benefit or
Stealing? . . . Lying: Is It Justifiable on the
Job? . . . Selling Out: When What You're
Expected to Do Violates Your Values . . .
Breaking the Law for Profit or Survival: Should
You Be a Party to It? . . . Whistle-Blowing:
When to Risk Your Job for a Principle

I once had a boss who occasionally gave me money from the company coffer to take my friends to lunch. At that point in my career, I couldn't afford to do much more than bring in a brown-bag lunch or buy a slice of pizza, so eating at some of the nicer restaurants in New York was a real treat. I knew that these lunches didn't fall under the category of "business," even though that's the impression the company accountants got from our receipts. My low salary allayed any twinges of guilt I felt about misrepresenting the way the money was really spent.

Many people would agree that these deluxe lunches were a job perk, but, if I had expanded the habit when I eventually was given my own expense account, I could easily have run up restaurant bills for lunches with friends in the hundreds of dollars each year. Small potatoes? In one respect, yes. There were plenty of other ways the company "legitimately" wasted much vaster sums. But if I had continued to raid the cookie jar, I could have fallen victim to what Professor John Matthews, who has taught ethics at the Harvard Business School, calls the "installment plan erosion of values."

It works this way. The first few times you cheat, you feel reticent; you don't want to get caught, and you feel slightly conscience-stricken about your actions. The more often you do it, however, the easier it is to trick yourself into believing that you're not hurting anyone, including yourself. A survey of 1,000 executives found that two thirds of them think people are occasionally unethical in their business dealings. Twenty-five percent believe that ethical standards can impede successful careers, while two thirds say that younger executives compromise their ethics "by the desire for wealth and material things." Executives also said that half of their acquaintances would bend the rules to achieve success if their actions had no victims.

You were no doubt faced with moral choices in college. But the consequences will matter more now, if only because the bottom line is your job.

Most of the ethical choices you will encounter at work will be small-time. You won't have to decide whether to use illegal aliens to keep your business alive or give a buyer a kickback. But you will have to decide whether you're going to make long-distance phone calls to your friends, tell white lies for your boss, or pad your expense account. You will have to contend with the pressure from your conscience, your peers, and your feelings of loyalty to your boss or the company.

A lot of questions are raised in this chapter; very few of them are answered. It's easy to speculate about your response to a moral dilemma, more difficult if you're actually faced with one. So save individual judgments for the real thing, but give some serious thought to the limits of what you can live with.

Freebies: Understanding Their True Cost

The most exciting freebie on my first job was an all-expense-paid trip from New York to Philadelphia aboard a top rock star's private plane. I was on my way to the premiere concert of his cross-country tour. After the concert, a party, complete with enough food and booze for several hundred people, was held on a riverboat. It was definitely a first-class perk.

I didn't feel compromised by accepting the invitation; the magazine I worked for didn't actually do concert reviews as such. If I had been a reviewer, however, I would have been in a difficult position. Suppose I thought the concert was awful? It would have been ungracious to pan it.

While journalists are most often the recipients of promotional freebies, there are plenty of other varieties aimed at people in other professions, the most common of which are free lunches (at expensive restaurants), a bottle of liquor, or a small present. Like product or promotional freebies, these niceties are intended to establish goodwill or a personal relationship with the client; sometimes they're a thank-you for a favor. While a freebie may seem on the up-and-up, the potential for abuse isn't far beneath the surface.

That's why some people categorically refuse any freebie that smacks of influence peddling. Other professionals accept what appear to be small innocuous gestures — flowers or a bottle of wine at Christmas. And some people feel they can judge each perk as it comes up.

The freebies that come your way in a first job aren't likely to be big ones and, like many of those I collected on my first job, may not interfere in any way with your job performance. The important thing, however, is to be able to recognize a freebie for what it is so that the choice you make won't affect your integrity or your employer's opinion of you. Remember, freebies aren't free at all. And you may end up compromising your professional reputation to pay for one.

Petty Theft on the Job: Fringe Benefit or Stealing?

When top executives who have been bilking their companies for tens of thousands of dollars get caught, most of us profess moral indignation. But the biggest nonviolent crime against American business is not embezzlement or securities fraud—it's employee pilferage. Between $15-billion and $25-billion is stolen each year.

Many people feel that, within certain limits, it's permissible and even expected to take items from their employers. The question is: Just where does one draw the line? It may seem logical to take home damaged merchandise that otherwise would be sent back to the manufacturer or thrown out, but what about "accidentally" damaging something so that you can "legitimately" take it? If using the company phone to make an overseas call to your brother doesn't faze you, why feel guilty if you "borrow" a piece of office equipment that was equal in price to the phone call?

A study by the American Management Association found that the will-I-get-caught factor was the biggest deterrent to petty theft. When you see that other people with whom you work steal and get away with it, or that your boss doesn't care, you may well feel you're losing out if you don't do likewise.

The AMA study also found that white-collar workers were just as likely as blue-collar workers to steal. Young, never-married employees were the worst culprits of all; possibly they had less to lose if they were fired. Dissatisfied employees, however, were more frequently involved in theft than were those who felt their employers were fair and ethical themselves. One of the most surprising findings was that people who took a lot said they were very concerned with self-improvement and meeting career goals.

In retail stores, the most common theft is misuse of the employee discount privilege; in manufacturing firms, it's raw materials used in production; in hospitals, supplies such as linens are the favorite take-home item.

The most abused privilege across the board is telephone calls. If you have a private office or aren't within earshot of your boss, it's pretty tempting to make those expensive long-distance phone calls during office hours. The cost of phone service, however, is a major expense for most employers.

Many employees are also light-fingered with office supplies. The first time Ellen Forster decided to take an office binder home, she waited until everyone had gone and slunk out with it concealed in a grocery bag. When she later found out that old-model binders were thrown out each year when the new models came in, her guilt disappeared, and she was able to apply a similar rationalization for the bigger items she later took.

One way to look at tape-and-stationery crimes is that, if your employer doesn't care, why should you? Or perhaps you feel that an occasional phone call or batch of stamps is no skin off anyone's back; it's the person who does it routinely who is out of line. That rationalization crumbles quickly in light of this fact: the cumulative result of nickel-and-dime crimes is higher prices for consumers. Few companies insure themselves against theft from the inside. In the case of businesses with small profit margins, employee theft can be a major factor in failure.

Some employers say they would fire a dishonest employee even if his offense were minor because they would feel unable to trust him with more important matters. Most have fewer qualms about dismissing someone new for such indiscretions than they would an experienced and otherwise honest employee.

Fudging on an Expense Account

While it may be some time before you are given your own expense account, you will no doubt discover that a number of people in your office consider it an extra bank account.

One of the most common rationalizations for padding is the I'm-not-paid-what-I'm-worth argument. Expense accounts are business expenses anyway, so the person who pads earns a more equitable salary, and, the argument goes, his employer never really feels the effect.

How can someone pad an expense account if all the receipts verifying the charges must be attached? The rules of creative accounting are actually quite simple. If you have paid for a meal in cash, you can write in any amount on the blank stub attached to the check. Or you might simply put in for a business lunch you never really took.

Many people who don't feel comfortable fictionalizing their expenses pocket extra money without actually taking it from their employers. Business travelers track down the most inexpensive air fares, cash in the more expensive company ticket, and put the difference in their wallet. Or they walk or take mass transportation to their destination and put in for a cab. Some people reason that, if they're willing to cut corners or bargain hunt, they should be the beneficiary of their efforts.

But if you choose to pass on the savings to your employer, the benefits that result may be more important than the money itself. At the very least, your employer will realize that you're resourceful and know how to budget money. He may appreciate the gesture, if only because so few other employees ever do it. If he has the option of sending you or someone else on a trip, he may send you because he knows you're more economical.

Padding your own expense account is one thing, but suppose you find discrepancies when you're doing your boss's expense account? If it's the first time the situation has come up, ask him how you should list the discrepancy. He may have forgotten to get a receipt, put an "extra" expense through to make up for an earlier one he forgot to note, or simply made a mistake. If, however, he tells you how to bury expenses and asks you to keep expense-account matters quiet, you'll be in a much tougher position. If you let him know you feel uncomfortable, he may ask someone else to do it or simply take over himself. But he may also resent your reluctance, which may hurt your relationship—and your future. It's usually not a good idea to bring your boss's expense-account habits to the attention of management unless the discrepancy involves thousands of dollars (or whatever amount you believe honesty is worth risking your job for).

Lying: Is It Justifiable on the Job?

George Langley, who works in a business where hundreds of thousands of dollars change hands in a single transaction, feels business is a giant game of Monopoly, complete with play money, bluff tactics, and good and bad rolls of the dice. He wouldn't think of lying to his close friends or family but has no qualms about misrepresenting himself to employers or clients when it's in his interest—or his company's—to do so. That kind of cavalier business attitude means operating with one set of values during working hours and another during your hours off the job. If you find it expeditious to lie to get ahead in your job, will you be tempted to play by the same rules in your personal life?

Chances are you'll be faced with one or more of the following job situations in which lying seems to be the easiest, and sometimes the most profitable, thing to do. What you can't predict when you're trying to make a decision is whether the lie will come back to haunt you, get out of control, or cause damage in ways you never suspected.

Lying to Get a Job

You have decided to look for a job while you wait to hear from the graduate schools to which you've applied. An employer who seems very interested in hiring you tells you that he wants to hire someone who is willing to make at least a two-year commitment.

You're torn. After all, your top priority is graduate school, and, if you're accepted (which you'll know within a few months), you would like to start as soon as you can. On the other hand, the job offer is tempting because the salary is good and the experience would be valuable. Being candid will ruin your chances. If you're honest, you may end up with a lower-paying, less interesting job. And where will you be if you don't get into graduate school?

It's usually easy telling that first lie because you don't know the employer and owe him nothing. But, by the time you get a go-ahead from a graduate school, you will have established a personal relationship; and, if your employer has given you a fair shake, you're going to feel like you're jumping ship. If you decide to cover your tracks by lying about your original intention, he may later learn of your misrepresentation, which can be an enormous liability if, in the future, you need his recommendation or have to do business with him. If you really think your boss deserves to be told the truth, you'll destroy his trust in you and probably disappoint him.

The moral of this scenario is that there are no easy choices, but before you make a decision that involves a to-lie-or-not-to-lie dilemma, ask yourself these questions:

- What are the alternatives to lying?
- What are the possible consequences to me if I lie or tell the truth?
- Who else might be hurt by my telling the truth or lying?
- Might another lie be necessary at a later time to prop up the first lie?
- How will I feel about myself if I lie?
- Does the cost of my being caught in a lie outweigh the benefit I hope to achieve?

Lying to Do a Good Job

Some professions are more susceptible to deceit than others, points out Sissela Bok in her book *Lying*. "Doctors, lawyers, journalists and military personnel may often face situations in which serious consequences seem avoidable only through deception . . . and wherever the opportunities for deceptions abound, rewards are high and time for considering alternatives often short."

One of Scott Holland's first reporting assignments was a human-interest story about the effect of a dying amusement park on people in the community. He spent a day interviewing people but still didn't feel he had gotten a good story. Rather than tell his editor he needed more time, he invented a character who was a combination of various people interviewed. The story was well received; in fact, several other papers picked it up as well. Scott was afraid he would be asked to do a follow-up and have to confess the person didn't exist. To his relief, that didn't happen, but his fear cured him of that particular dubious journalistic practice.

Some people would argue that what Scott did was fine as long as he didn't create any false impressions in the process. Others would say that that kind of artistic license belongs only to fiction writers. But the more important moral question is whether it was the right thing to do under the circumstances. Scott could have asked for an extension of his deadline, which might have altered his boss's opinion of his reporting abilities. Or he could have written a story based on what he did have, which might have been acceptable but not as good. In a sense, the white lie was the riskiest option, since, if he had been found out, his professional reputation might have gone down the tubes.

It's particularly difficult to decide what to do in a first job because you don't have the judgment to know the consequences of various alternatives, and the pressure to appear competent is strong. You have to decide how far you're willing to go when the effects of your lies may be worse than the criticism you're trying to avoid or will scarcely be worth risking for the kudos you're trying to collect.

Lying to Cover for Your Boss

Few people think twice about telling white lies for their bosses. Telling a caller your boss is in conference when he really just doesn't want to take the call is no big deal. It's an expected part of the relationship. While it's rare that anyone suffers as a result of a fib, outright lies to clients, other employees, or the management of the company can have serious consequences.

Are you responsible because of your complicity in a cover-up or in misrepresenting the truth? To the extent that your going along with the lie was voluntary, it follows that you have to share the blame and the possible consequences. But suppose you went along only because you didn't want to jeopardize your relationship with your boss? That's a much trickier situation, since you were following someone else's orders. But just how far should loyalty go?

John DeAngelis worked for a buyer who instructed him not to talk to anyone else in the company about what went on in their department. John soon realized why — his boss was putting false information on inventory sheets. When John was asked by an internal auditor to check his boss's sheets against the auditor's report, he didn't know whether to protect his boss by saying the two checked out okay or to bring up the discrepancies and risk his boss's anger. He got out of the immediate dilemma by mentioning the matter to his boss, who lied his own way out of it. John eventually asked to be transferred to another department.

Being loyal to your boss has many advantages, especially if he is a mover. But your obligation to remain loyal ends when the behavior or action you're being asked to support is harmful or potentially harmful to others. If you operate on the premise that his lies will never be discovered, you may be hitching your ambition to a dubious star.

Lying to Conform

Don Lasky was surprised to hear his boss, the store manager, tell a customer that the reason advertised merchandise wasn't in stock was that the delivery truck had encountered weather problems. When Don asked about it, his boss said he made up the excuse because he was too busy to deal with a rain check.

Social worker Lea Mikulski was shocked when the director of her agency told her not to enter certain information into the record when she visited welfare clients since the agency couldn't keep clients who lost their welfare benefits.

In the introduction to *Lying*, Sissela Bok writes, "Existing deceptive practices ... can make it difficult not to conform ... few are encouraged to consider such choices in schools and colleges or in their working life." It's particularly tough to know the right thing to do in your first job because you have nothing against which to compare your employer's behavior. Often, the only available gauge is whether "the way things are done around here" conflicts with your personal values.

Businesspeople say that "strategic misrepresentation," deliberately holding back information when it is to their advantage, is not uncommon in sales. Some salespeople in their first jobs, says the manager of a computer company, make the mistake of thoroughly answering all of the customers' questions. The answers to technical ones can be misinterpreted and cost a sale.

In a *Harvard Business Review* survey, most of the executives responding said that an employee who objected to falsifying company records for the benefit of the company should be reinstated if his immediate boss fired him. But only 78 percent of those executives said that they believed that would be the probable outcome at their company.

Whether to go along with the way your company does business or buck the system is a difficult choice. If there isn't room for you to follow your conscience within the system, the only way to feel comfortable may be to find a similar job with a company whose practices you find more palatable.

Selling Out: When What You're Expected to Do Violates Your Values

The business world, you'll soon discover, is often cold and somewhat ruthless; time and money often take precedence over the humanitarian choice or the "right thing to do." The first time you object to something you feel is wrong and correctable, don't be surprised if you're labeled naive. But that should not deter you from questioning similar situations in the future.

It's important, however, to learn the distinction between flexibility and compromise. Being flexible means accepting certain inevitabilities about the way business is done and is essential to surviving in the 9-to-5 world. Compromise, on the other hand, means taking unnecessary shortcuts that may be potentially harmful to employees or customers. It may boost your career, but it may also erode your integrity.

The bottom line is: if you're unhappy with yourself because of the choices you're being forced to make to keep your job, you may have to find a more comfortable niche. Here are some of the sellout situations you're likely to be faced with on a first job, and how some people handled them.

Questioning a Superior's Judgment

Sarah Underwood, whose first job was with a housing agency, accompanied one of her bosses to a boarded-up housing site to determine whether rehabilitation was an option. When the maintenance crew didn't show up to open the building, her superior crowbarred his way in. After they completed the inspection, Sarah refused to leave until he boarded up the entranceway, which left an elevator shaft exposed. Just then the maintenance crew arrived, and the problem was solved. Her boss resented Sarah's correcting him, though, and got back at her by routinely disapproving her work from then on. She finally felt compelled to file an official complaint, but her boss was transferred to a different division before any formal action was taken.

Reporter Dorothy Powell was shocked when her editor killed a story she had written on the opening of a grocery warehouse in the Southern city where she worked. The reason: the warehouse wasn't planning on advertising in the paper, and her editor was afraid other food stores might cancel their ads if "free publicity" were given to a competitor who was undercutting their prices. Even though her editor's judgment violated every journalistic principle she had been taught in school, Dorothy said nothing. She was afraid that would be the end of her job.

If you choose to quarrel with a person whose judgment you feel is wrong (and who has control over your job), your objections are unlikely to be appreciated, even if the other person knows you're right and he's wrong. Don't come on like a knight in shining armor by pointing out the wrongness of a boss's action; try to win your point by making polite observations and bringing him around to thinking that a change of heart is really consistent with his own ideas. This approach requires a fairly sophisticated level of manipulation, but it never hurts to start practicing early in your career. One last hint: don't pick on the small things that probably don't make a difference to anyone but you. Save your energy for the big issues, or you'll earn a reputation as someone who's unrealistic and hard to get along with.

Disagreeing with Your Employer's Philosophy

Should you feel like you're selling out because you work for a company whose philosophy you don't support or whose name is associated with something you strongly oppose? Most corporations engage in a variety of what many would consider antisocial behaviors: contributing to the pollution of the environment or perpetuating sexist or racist practices. And you don't necessarily escape that problem by working for a small employer. Your boss may belong to a private business club that excludes women, blacks, Jews, or all three. He may contribute money, support, or the company's name to causes or candidates that you strenuously object to.

What you'll have to decide is how much your own work contributes to the profitability of the company or the product or service to which you object—and whether you can live with that. Of course, if you know it's the cumulative effect of work like yours that makes it possible for your employer to continue his work, you may have plenty of sleepless nights.

Even in a tight economy, there is room for freedom of choice. There are plenty of unsung heroes who make decisions on principle—and you shouldn't feel pressured to compromise your own values because your peers can tolerate conditions that bother you.

Refusing an Assignment

- A female associate is asked to research a sex-discrimination complaint brought by a group of women against their employer. The dilemma: her client is the employer whose actions she must help defend.

- A junior ad agency artist is asked to join a team designing an ad campaign for a new brand of cigarettes. The dilemma: he personally disapproves of smoking.

- A nurse is instructed by the attending doctor to disregard the request of a patient's family and give him higher doses of medication, which is not crucial to his recovery. The dilemma: does she comply with the order, refuse it, or do it but inform the patient's family?

What choice do you have when you're asked to do something that isn't wrong in itself but violates your values? If you refuse the order outright, you may be fired for insubordination. The opposite response ensures smooth sailing, but the resulting internal crises may send you to a shrink.

There is, however, another alternative. You can explain your feelings to your boss and ask him if he thinks your beliefs might in any way compromise your role in the project. That gives him the opportunity to put someone else on in your place and gets you off the hook. If he asks you to go ahead anyway, you'll have to either shelve your personal feelings or tell your employer that you cannot in conscience carry out his request—and let the chips fall where they may.

Breaking the Law for Profit or Survival: Should You Be a Party to It?

The most publicized corporate crimes are committed by people in positions of power. But you can be put in the position of an accomplice, or worse. Consider these cases:

- Pat Kaiser handled fund-raising for her boss, a politician, and often turned down cash contributions that were over the legal cash amount, even when that meant a smaller contribution. She knew that if any discrepancy were discovered, she might end up damaging her boss's career and her own.

- Instead of a raise, Tom Engwars was offered the use of a new company car—all expenses paid. He was asked to "keep it quiet." Since his job rarely required using a car, it was basically for his own personal use. Both he and his company profited from the arrangement since he didn't have to pay additional tax on his "raise" and his company could write it off as a business expense and do the same.

- Mark Quinn was asked by his boss to put through a payment to an official of a foreign government with which his company hoped to do business. Mark told his boss he didn't feel right about paying the bribe. His boss's response was to give the task to someone else.

Each of the above examples involves a possible crime. While it's true that most minor infractions and some serious ones are never uncovered by the authorities, the law enforcement investigation of white-collar crime has been stepped up and the penalties for convicted companies stiffened. Fewer unethical business practices are tolerated nowadays. For instance, bribing foreign officials to establish business relations with their countries became illegal in 1977 with the passage of the Foreign Corrupt Practices Act. And plenty of under-the-table deals are snagged when a company is hit by the fickle finger of fate — the random IRS audit. The point is: if you work for a company or boss whose business dealings are shady, you might get caught unknowingly or involuntarily in the middle of an illegal escapade.

Take the worst possible scenario. Your company's activities come under scrutiny by the local district attorney's office. You may be called upon to identify signatures, relate conversations you overheard, or even testify against your superiors. That's a no-win situation if you still work for the company. If you don't tell what you know, you could be indicted for perjury; if you do, you can almost assuredly count yourself out of a job. If you did your employer's dirty work for him (even out of ignorance), you may be personally liable for your actions. When indictments are flying, everyone is out to save his own neck, and any earlier promises of protection may be promptly abandoned. In rare situations, you may even be made a scapegoat.

Probably even more important (if only because it's a bigger risk) is what can happen to your professional reputation if you engage in illicit or borderline business activities or work for a company that does so routinely. If, for example, you work for a company that encourages its sales force to use dubious high-pressure tactics, you're faced with potential problems. Since the sales techniques you're learning aren't accepted by more reputable companies, you may have trouble using your experience as a stepping-stone to a better job. Most companies are aware of their competitors' ways of doing business.

If you discover that your employer routinely engages in illegal business practices, the only sure way to keep your own reputation from being muddied is to ask for a transfer to a different division or to leave the company. If the violations are minor or if you personally aren't offended by this bending or breaking of the rules, you may feel the risks are worth taking.

Whistle-Blowing: When to Risk Your Job for a Principle

Suppose you find out that:
- Your company is dumping chemical wastes with unacceptable levels of toxic material into a nearby river.

- The recommendations concerning a defect in a product aren't acted upon by your division.
- Information about potential safety hazards to employees in a division of your company is withheld from them.

Should you say anything? And to whom?

This is the dilemma of the would-be whistle-blower, the person who has access to information that is potentially harmful to his employer. The would-be whistle-blower is understandably wary of spilling the beans because he feels it's not his place to speak up or because he is concerned that, if he does, he will jeopardize his job.

Jennifer Bascas, who worked for a government agency, was aware that her boss was harassing employees whose political views differed drastically from his own; they were given the worst assignments and denied earned promotions. When a labor union that represented the employees asked Jennifer to testify before a Senate subcommittee to divulge what she knew about her boss's wrongdoings, she agreed; as a result of her testimony and others', her boss was investigated by the justice department.

Jennifer's position wasn't jeopardized, but that isn't always the case. The documented cases of whistle-blowers show that many are harassed or fired by their employers. Some are blackballed in their fields. And sometimes their speaking out accomplishes no appreciable change.

When you're inexperienced, it's often difficult to make an informed judgment about the legality or ethics of corporate behavior. On the other hand, some actions are so blatantly out of line that anyone would have a gut feeling they're wrong. In his book *Whistle Blowing,* Ralph Nader writes, "The willingness and ability of insiders to blow the whistle is the last line of defense ordinary citizens have against the denial of their rights and the destruction of their interests by secretive and powerful institutions."

Before you decide to say anything, be sure your information is complete and accurate. If you're not sure whether the practices are objectionable, ask the opinions of some of the more experienced people in your department. If they confirm your suspicions, you may want to approach the subject diplomatically with your boss, again by asking an innocuous question — Why are things done this way? — to find out his feelings. You may also be able to find out whether management is aware of the problem and chooses to ignore it. Document the history of the problem, and make copies of documents that support your claims.

It's smart to get legal advice; you can start by contacting a local American Civil Liberties Union office. Some seventeen states have whistle-blower protection statutes, and the majority protect state government employees. But these laws do not insulate you from the persecution and job difficulties that follow. A survey of 100 whistle-blowers by psychologist and one-time whistle-blower Donald R. Soeken found that:

- More than 80 percent felt their initial actions were unsuccessful and had to resort to other strategies.

- All but one reported retaliation, including harassment from superiors and peers, monitoring of their activities and office telephone, demotion, loss of responsibilities, and firing.
- All reported suffering moderate to extreme stress as a result of their actions.
- Seventeen percent lost their homes because of their actions, 15 percent said whistle-blowing contributed to a divorce, 8 percent filed for bankruptcy, and 10 percent attempted suicide.

Given the inevitable personal and career difficulties you may face by doing what you feel is right, consider what you hope to achieve and how it may affect you before you proceed. If, after a careful fact-finding and soul-searching mission, you feel that the problem is serious and that you cannot in good conscience do nothing, consider whom to contact, and whether to do it anonymously, overtly, or resign before you report the problem.

11

Discrimination

Job Inequities: When They're Illegal . . . Taming Office Wolves: How to Handle Sexual Harassment . . . Keeping Your Cool: What to Do If You Suspect You're a Victim . . . Making a Complaint Official: How to Win Respect Rather Than Resentment . . . Filing a Suit: How and When to Do It

In recent years, many employers have made genuine efforts to correct company policies and practices that deliberately or inadvertently discriminate against women and members of minority groups. Many large companies instituted affirmative action offices to deal with employee complaints and designed programs that would encourage women and minorities to get the training necessary to move into jobs in which they had not traditionally been well represented.

The most forward-thinking of organizations are beginning to realize that they will be at a competitive disadvantage unless they nurture the careers of women and minority employees, who are expected to constitute 85 percent of the new employees in the nineties. The steps being taken by companies who are "managing diversity," as the practice is often referred to, include conducting workshops on understanding and valuing differences; forming special-interest groups that provide regular feedback to management about problems and solutions; and overhauling their recruitment, performance-evaluation, and promotion systems.

Nonetheless, there is still plenty of job discrimination. Much of it is subtle because employers do not want to invite legal suits or adverse publicity. But it can be as overt as what happened to Ann Hopkins, who successfully sued her employer, Price Waterhouse, in a precedent-setting case when she was denied partnership in 1982. Several male partners put her nomination on hold because they felt she was too "macho" and in need of a "charm school," despite the fact that she had the best record for developing new business and bringing in multimillion-dollar contracts among the eighty-eight candidates (all male except her) up for promotion.

In 1989, the U.S. Supreme Court held that Price Waterhouse had based its decision in part on unlawful sexual stereotyping—a violation of Title VII of the Civil Rights Act of 1964, which bars job discrimination on the basis of sex, race, religion, or national origin. The result of this decision, say legal experts, is that it will be easier for victims to win job discrimination cases, and employers will have to be more careful about whom they allow to make important personnel decisions.

Job Inequities: When They're Illegal

Life is unfair, and so is the working world. A lot of things will happen to you that you may not think are "right." But just because you're treated differently or aren't given the same breaks as your peers doesn't mean you're a victim of discrimination.

Simply put, the law says you cannot be denied a job or fair treatment on the job because of your sex, race, religion, or national origin, if you work for:

- A private employer of fifteen or more people
- State or local government
- A public or private educational institution
- A public or private employment agency
- A labor union with fifteen or more members

Although that may sound clear-cut, the interpretation of "fair treatment" is often a bone of contention, which is why a plethora of complaints have ended up in the courts. If you are a woman, in order for an employer's action to be illegal, he must have treated you differently from your male peers, and the treatment must have had a negative impact on your job or career. If what happens to you is an isolated instance (e.g., other women have been admitted to training programs in the past or held positions of responsibility in the company), it will be much tougher to prove your case.

The most common problems women are likely to face in looking for work or in their first job are:

- Being offered a job only in a traditionally female area, even though their qualifications are the same as men hired into different capacities
- Being denied the promotional opportunities available to men on their level
- Having restricted use of company facilities to which men have full access
- Being subjected to sexual demands from their male coworkers or boss that negatively affect their job or career

Title VII and the Equal Employment Opportunity Act of 1972 are the two major federal laws that protect you against job discrimination. Most states also have fair employment practices and equal pay laws that protect your rights.

While it's difficult to fight a one-person battle against an employer's sexist or racist practices, there are things you can do to protect yourself from becoming a victim. Most important is to avoid projecting a defensive attitude, especially if you are the only woman or minority person on your level. If you have a chip on your shoulder, you're a natural target for a boss with prejudices. Don't segregate yourself into a job ghetto by associating primarily with people of your own sex or race. Cultivate good relationships with other colleagues, particularly ones on higher levels. Their support and advice can be invaluable if you're later faced with a discriminatory situation.

Note: Although much of the language used in this section is written for a female reader, the advice on how to handle a discriminatory situation also applies to members of minority groups.

Taming Office Wolves: How to Handle Sexual Harassment

Nadine Eskell's first job seemed like a golden opportunity. She was hired as an assistant to a top television correspondent, a man who was her professional idol. Her responsibilities included research, scriptwriting, and traveling to help cover stories. The job also promised the experience she needed to eventually become a production assistant. Her dream job turned into a nightmare overnight. During her first week on the job, Nadine and her boss went out to dinner and he propositioned her. She had thought he chose her over the other job candidates because she was the best-qualified person for the job. She was devastated when she realized that being a tall, good-looking blonde had been her most important credential. Nadine tried to put him off by telling him that a sexual involvement might impair their working together.

Over the next few weeks, he persisted in his efforts to get her into bed. He threatened her by extending the trial period of her job. She didn't want to lose the job, so she tried to humor him without giving in. The sexual tug-of-war went on for six months, until Nadine was added permanently to the company's payroll. But her boss played the role of rejected suitor—he humiliated her in front of her coworkers, offered her "services" to clients (to her embarrassment and theirs), and ordered her to do menial tasks.

In the beginning, Nadine's coworkers thought she had slept her way into the position (her boss led them to believe that was the case) and would have nothing to do with her. Eventually, they became aware of the real situation, and, although they sympathized with her, no one had the clout to challenge his treatment of her.

Nadine tolerated the situation for fifteen months to get the experience she felt she needed to transfer to another job in the company. Her chances were dashed when the executive producer of a different division, who had considered hiring her, got a less than complimentary recommendation from her boss. It was his final revenge.

While Nadine was subjected to one of the most extreme forms of sexual harassment, her story is not an isolated one. Despite laws prohibiting sexual harassment in the workplace, the incidence of such behavior has not decreased, according to a 1987 survey of federal employers by the U.S. Merit Systems Protection Board. Forty-two percent of the women and 14 percent of the men surveyed claimed they had been victims of unwanted and uninvited sexual attention between 1985 and 1987 — almost the identical percentages cited in a similar study done seven years earlier.

Women in their first jobs are particularly susceptible to being taken advantage of; no matter how much experience they've had dealing with aggressive men, they don't know how to put off a man who controls their job future.

In the most blatant kind of sexual harassment, your boss demands you make the choice between giving sexual favors and losing your job. Some bosses with casting-couch mentalities are subtle in their approach. They don't actually demand, they insinuate. Soon after she was hired as a sales representative, Jeannette Wilson's boss told her if she had any problems to be sure and stop by his office — after 5. If individual meetings were scheduled with members of the sales staff, hers was the last of the day — when few other people were around. He created opportunities for something to happen, and, when she didn't "come through" after several months, he fired her. One of the other salesmen had warned her that that was the reason she had been hired. But Jeannette felt there was nothing she could have done to change what happened short of acquiescing; neither did she feel she had any recourse, because she couldn't "prove" that was the reason she was fired.

Even more common is the boss who promises job promotions in return for sexual favors. Sixty-three women employees at the Housing and Urban Development Department said they had received that invitation; the majority of the 30 percent who consented did in fact benefit in advancement or pay. Most of those who declined claimed they were passed over for promotion.

Sexual harassment need not involve a threat to your job; it may simply make you feel uncomfortable. If you work in an office in which there is a macho mentality, you may be subjected to dirty jokes, obscenities (which may be directed at you), double entendres, or "affectionate" pats on the behind. You'll have to decide how much you're willing to go along with — a lot will depend on whether it is the malicious or no-harm-intended type.

Sexual harassment on the job has been a closet issue for a long time. Many women were too embarrassed to admit the problem and felt that there was nothing that could be done about it, while men often see nothing wrong with sexual overtures and defend one another's actions.

There are, however, ways to fend off unwanted advances and put verbal harassment in its place. It took Valerie Salter almost a year to convince the head of her division that she didn't want to go to bed with him. He had a ladies'-man reputation, and soon after she started her first job he asked her along on business trips to which others on her level were not invited. Several times, he actually tried to force himself on her. She refused but continued to be friendly with him. Rather than feeling immediately rejected, he took her resistance as a challenge. Although she benefited in many ways from his attention — she was invited to important meetings and had status because of her easy access to him — it sometimes worked against her. Men on higher levels resented her "rapport" with him; even her immediate boss admitted he didn't give her the highest possible performance rating because he felt she was too friendly with the division head. When he finally got the message that she wasn't interested in a sexual relationship, he let up on his advances. Their relationship remained amicable in part because she had had time to build a solid track record on the job.

If you're faced with a boss or coworker who is harassing you, here are some approaches you might consider using:

1. *Ignore the remarks or advances.* Refusing to recognize offensive behavior or simply changing the subject shows that you aren't interested and do not find the person amusing. The cold-shoulder routine will eventually discourage some types of office wolves.

2. *Make light of the situation or try to laugh it off.* If you make it clear you don't take the offer seriously, he may back off rather than risk being rejected. The more forward Romeos, however, may think you're being coy. You'll have to use stronger techniques with them.

3. *Object on professional grounds.* Being straightforward in your refusal — "I think our working relationship might be jeopardized by our becoming that intimate" — makes the rejection less personal. It's the situation, and not the person, that makes the idea unworkable.

4. *Limit his opportunities to make overtures.* Cut down on or eliminate small talk, and avoid being alone with him unless it's necessary for business reasons.

5. *Tone down any "encouraging" signals.* Some men complain that women flaunt their sexuality by the way they dress. In some cases, that criticism is warranted; in others, it would make no difference how businesslike the dress. Your best bet is to save sexy clothes for after working hours.

6. *Find out if other women in the office have problems with him.* They may be able to give you advice on how they handled him, or several of you may want to confront him as a group and tell him his behavior is out of line.

7. *Make a loud refusal — one that can be heard by others in the office.* This tactic is risky, and, since the point is to embarrass him, it shouldn't be used unless all else has failed.

If your boss (or the man in question) won't take no for an answer and your refusal has a negative impact on your work — that is, it affects your reputation or credibility or holds you back from promotions or raises — you should take steps to protect yourself. Tell him that unless he stops bothering you, you plan to make an official complaint. If he continues despite your warning, talk to his boss or the person in the company who handles employee complaints (see the section on complaints in this chapter). Keep in mind that, once you take this step, you should be prepared to leave your job, since management may back him up if he is a valuable employee.

If you are fired from your job because you refuse to give in or voluntarily resign because you cannot tolerate the situation, you may be able to collect unemployment insurance. California and Wisconsin have enacted legislation that provides unemployment compensation under those conditions, and in other states courts have ruled that sexual harassment is an unacceptable working condition, which entitles the victim to unemployment pay. Check with your local unemployment office to find out how it would rule on such a case or with a local women's rights group for their advice and help. Forty-five percent of the women who took their complaints of sexual harassment to federal court between 1974 and 1986 won them, according to a study conducted by David E. Terpstra, professor of management at the University of Idaho.

The cases that succeeded were most often those in which at least one of the following conditions was true:

- Forceful advances that consisted of unwanted physical contact such as kissing or fondling were made.

- Witnesses heard the threats or saw the action.

- The victim kept a written record of conversations and behavior or kept notes sent by the harasser to her.

- Management failed to act after receiving a complaint from the victim.

If all these conditions are met, says Terpstra, you have a 70 percent chance of winning.

Keeping Your Cool: What to Do If You Suspect You're a Victim

- Despite your requests, you're not given assignments that require overnight trips, although your male colleagues are. You suspect the reason is that your boss doesn't approve of women traveling alone.

- Your employer tells you he can't promise to hold open a position for you if you take a maternity leave of several months.

- You want to leave your secretarial position for a management-trainee program. Your employer tells you that you don't have the right qualifications, but you know of men in the program whose credentials are no better than yours.

All of the above cases could be violations of antidiscrimination laws, but if you find yourself in a similar situation, it would be premature to accuse your employer of discrimination before you investigate all the facts. He may not be deliberately plotting against you; he may be unaware of the legal implications of his actions.

The first step is to talk to him about the situation and ask him to explain his reasons. It's better to ask frank questions than to immediately escalate matters into a confrontation; that only puts him in a defensive position. You might, for example, ask what you could do that would make a difference. If he hasn't given the matter much thought, he may see the unfairness of his actions and make changes or investigate it further.

If you don't agree with his reasons or his appraisal of the situation, don't be afraid to disagree. But keep your criticisms objective and your emotions under control. If your boss seems to understand your point of view but says there isn't anything he can do about it right now, ask him specifically how he intends to handle the situation in the future. You'll have to judge for yourself whether he's simply trying to put you off or whether he's sincere about his promises. Immediately after your talk, write down your questions and his answers so that you will have a record of the conversation. In the event that you eventually make an official complaint, any kind of documented evidence will be to your advantage.

If you get no satisfaction, you may want to seek advice from a higher-ranking women with whom you're friendly. It also might be worthwhile to check with other women in the company to see if they have experienced similar problems and what they did about them.

If the problem persists, your only recourse may be to take up the matter with your boss's boss. Before you do, explain to your boss why you feel that it's your only alternative. Don't pose it as a threat; most middle-level managers will bend over backward to avoid being accused of discrimination. Once he realizes you're not going to let the matter drop, he may rethink his decision. If, however, the inequity is one that is consistent with company policy, your boss would be sticking his neck out to go against it. Whether or not he takes that risk depends on whether he thinks you deserve a fairer shake and how much clout he has. If, however, he refuses to have anything more to do with it, discuss your complaint with his boss. Explain the problem objectively and calmly without sounding accusatory. Emphasize your commitment to the company and to doing a good job.

Making a Complaint Official: How to Win Respect Rather Than Resentment

If your supervisor's boss sides with him, the next step is to bring your complaint to the attention of management. It's important to give the situation a chance to rectify itself. If you didn't get as big a raise as your male colleague, but your boss says that was because he wasn't convinced you deserved it and promises to reevaluate your performance in three months, insisting on a more immediate reappraisal would be jumping the gun. Making an official complaint is an emotionally draining experience. And you will have to put even more effort into your work once you file a complaint, since your superiors may feel threatened and may be on the lookout for reasons to criticize your performance.

Before you talk to management, put your complaint in writing. Include all relevant factual material: when the alleged discriminatory episode occurred; when you met with your boss (and his boss) and what was said; copies of your performance review (if your company gives them). Discuss why you feel you deserved the promotion, raise, or training opportunity. The better prepared you are, the stronger your case will be: it will show management that you're serious about making the complaint, that you've thought the situation through, and that you've taken the steps necessary to having your complaint investigated.

The most common complaint mechanism is a talk with a senior executive who functions as a formal or informal ombudsman. If no such position exists in your company, you might discuss the problem with the personnel staffer whose job it is to investigate grievances and report to top management. If your company has an affirmative action office or grievance committee, discussing the situation with the Equal Employment Opportunity (EEO) officer is your best bet. In some companies, however, the EEO officer has no clout — and even if he or she is on your side, you may have a tough uphill battle ahead. If you belong to a union, talk to your steward or representative. (Since many unions are dominated by white males, there's always the risk he may not be sympathetic, in which case you'll have to go to a higher-ranking official of the union or to a local human rights agency.)

Once you make your complaint official, don't expect miracles overnight. It will take time — weeks, and possibly even months — before the matter is discussed with others in management and your boss. It is a good idea to check back periodically to make sure that the person handling your complaint is working on it.

How the situation is resolved will depend to a large extent on your handling of it. If you're belligerent, demanding, and threatening, it will be more difficult for your company's management to objectively examine the basis of your complaint. Companies do not lightly side with an employee against one of its managers. But if you proceed calmly and persistently, it's more likely your company will take you seriously and thoroughly investigate your complaint.

Filing a Suit: How and When to Do It

Taking your complaint outside the company is a last resort. It can be time-consuming, costly, and sometimes ineffective. If, however, your company's management gives you no satisfaction despite repeated efforts to negotiate alternatives, you shouldn't hesitate to take further steps.

Collect all the information you have that supports your case — memos and letters you wrote to your boss or the company's management and their responses, your diary of the incidents of discrimination.

Contact the local human rights commission (it's usually listed under "City of _____" in your phone book) or your state's local fair employment practices agency (look under "State of _____" in the phone book). Working with one of these two agencies is your best bet, since it will cost you nothing but time. If neither option is available, you can also get free help by contacting the nearest district office of the Equal Employment Opportunity Commission. After you file your complaint (a written document), let your employer know that you have done it. It's better that he find out from you than from the agency you have filed with. And it gives him one last chance to cooperate. Be polite and forthright; there's nothing to be gained from sounding self-righteous or threatening.

Hiring a private lawyer is faster but of course more expensive. A local women's rights group such as the National Organization of Women can give you the name of a lawyer qualified to handle discrimination cases or tell you about lower-cost services that are available through local law schools or other community organizations.

Many lawyers opted to take sex-discrimination and sexual harassment cases to state rather than federal court during the 1980s. The reason? Many state statutes allow the victim who wins her case to collect for mental anguish and invasion of privacy, while Title VII only allows for collection of back pay (and reinstatement in the job, which many victims do not want). Another benefit: many state civil rights acts allow a complainant to get a jury trial, which is not the case in federal court under Title VII, according to Darien McWhirter, a lawyer and the author of *Your Rights at Work*.

Whether you pursue matters on your own or put yourself in the hands of the government, you will have to come up with evidence. In the case of job inequities, you must show that company policy or your boss's behavior amounted to treating you differently because of your sex, race, or religion. It's much easier to prove discrimination if you can establish what seems to be a pattern of discrimination — that a smaller percentage of qualified women or members of minority groups are admitted to training programs, for example.

In the case of sexual harassment, you must prove that you were sexually coerced, that you resisted, that your refusal negatively affected your job, and that members of the opposite sex were not coerced.

It's usually best not to discuss your plans with anyone else in the office. They may later be asked to testify, and you don't want to give them information that ultimately could be used against you.

If the situation isn't likely to be resolved in a short time, you may want to consider transferring to a different division of the company or finding an entirely new job. You can almost count on the fact that you won't be promoted, and since you are openly disputing your boss, he may make things very unpleasant for you — even though outright harassment of an employee who has filed a complaint is illegal.

Finally, be prepared to see the matter through. You will make it tougher for the people who come after you if you decide to drop your complaint because you've found a better job or gotten tired of legal delays.

12

Moving On

Promotion: How Soon Can You Expect One? . . .
Job Dissatisfaction: Knowing When to Leave . . .
Your Second Job: What to Look For . . .
Changing Fields: How Difficult Is It? . . .
Getting Fired: It's Not the End of the World

I worked in my first job as an editorial assistant for thirteen months. Even though my responsibilities expanded — after four months I began writing a monthly column — I didn't think there was much chance of becoming a staff writer in the foreseeable future. So I left.

Only 5 percent of all college grads get that impatient and leave within their first year, but close to half change employers within four to five years.

There is no proper length of time to spend in Job One. If your responsibilities have not significantly changed or expanded after twelve to eighteen months, you may have slipped into a job rut. Before you begin looking for a new job to get your career rolling again, it's a good idea to talk to your boss about expanding your responsibilities or consider making a job move within your company. Employers say that you will have an easier time marketing yourself in Job Two if you have earned a promotion on your first job.

Even if that's the case, looking for your second job can be difficult if you have resigned. After three months of trying to support myself as a free-lance writer I decided I didn't enjoy the insecurity and actively began looking for my second job. It took me almost five months to find it, during which time my ego underwent a serious bruising. I was caught in a dilemma common to second-job seekers — overqualified for many jobs (I had a portfolio of articles) and without the experience (at age 22) to be seriously considered for a higher than entry-level position.

Before you decide to move on, it's a good idea to reappraise your situation and your goals and investigate your options.

Promotion: How Soon Can You Expect One?

Earning a promotion isn't as straightforward as earning a high grade in college. Turning in a great performance doesn't have the guaranteed effect that preparing a terrific term paper does. That's because getting ahead has as much to do with fate as it has to do with competence. Although there's nothing you can do to influence most external events, there are ways to enhance your position should fate smile on you.

Before you start pitching for more challenging assignments, make sure you've got what the job takes. Don't just guess; ask people who have done it before which skills they feel are necessary to do a good job. If you've had no experience using those skills, start volunteering for projects that might provide an opportunity.

Knowing the "right" people can be important to being considered for a promotion. If your accomplishments aren't known by anyone except your boss, you have to rely on him to speak on your behalf; and even a good boss is sometimes reluctant to lose a good employee, or doesn't take the time to tip you off to opportunities for which you might qualify. It's up to you to develop a reputation among people who can influence your career. If you have been keeping a low profile, you'll have to work at raising it. When people become aware of who you are, the quality of your work, and your interests, it's more likely that your name will be suggested when an opening comes up.

Developing competence and visibility takes time; it's unrealistic to expect that you will move out of an entry-level job after six weeks or even six months on the job. Most people in their first jobs report that they were not given a significant increase in responsibility until they had been on the job between one and two years. From the employer's point of view there are several reasons why this much time is necessary:

- It's expensive for an employer to hire and train a new person in a job, so the longer the turnover between people, the less expensive it is.
- Moving an employee up much faster than usual is bound to create resentment in other employees.
- It's easier to expand a job description than to formally promote you — and a good way of testing how you will do.

Even if you've been in a job long enough to be considered promotable, you may have to wait for someone to leave. And even then, there's no way of predicting what management will do. You may be the logical successor, but don't be surprised if management decides to consider other people as well.

Nine months after Gail Kislevitz began working as a personnel assistant in a bank, her boss left. She was the only person who knew how to do his job, and she applied for it, but management wanted to interview other candidates as well. Gail assumed responsibility for the department and gradually moved into her former boss's office with her manager's approval. (That helped her "secure" her position.) Gail handled the responsibilities of the job well and thereby made herself the clear choice.

If you feel frustrated by the constraints of your job and no better ones become available, talk to your boss about expanding your responsibilities. He may be aware of opportunities that you are not, or be able to suggest ways for you to broaden the scope of your job.

There is nothing wrong with actively pursuing more responsibility, as long as you do not demand it or put your employer in an untenable position. Joe Tabacco was able to move more quickly than usual from junior trial attorney to an intermediate level by slowly incorporating the responsibilities of the more advanced job into his work. He took them a step at a time, making sure his boss knew of and approved of what he was doing. Once he proved that he could handle the responsibilities, he got the money and title for the job he already was doing.

If you've exhausted all the possibilities for moving up within your company, investigating job possibilities elsewhere will give you a fair idea of whether you're premature in looking for advancement. You may even be able to find out which skill areas you need to strengthen before you can expect to land a better job.

Job Dissatisfaction: Knowing When to Leave

Only a handful of people are very satisfied with their first jobs. The vast majority become disenchanted because they aren't able to use their skills or see little chance for moving up—two factors essential to job satisfaction.

Your feelings about your job will fluctuate from week to week and day to day, and in a crisis-filled business from hour to hour. But how you feel about your job at any given moment is not as important as your gut sense of whether it's working out and whether in fact it is a stepping-stone.

It ordinarily takes months to know whether a job really is right for you. The exception is the job in which you don't feel comfortable from Day One. If that feeling grows, it's probably smart to make a quick exit. Androc Kislevitz felt that way three times within seven months. He knew he wanted a job in the communication field, but he wasn't sure exactly what. He worked as a copy boy at a daily newspaper for six weeks, as an editorial assistant at a book publishing firm for five months, and as a receptionist at an advertising agency for five weeks. He felt most at home in the last job, but, having found the right field, he wanted to learn all about it right away. He left to get a master's degree in advertising and netted three interesting job offers when he was graduated.

It's often hard to figure out just how much progress you're making or even how satisfied you are, with no comparable experience. If, however, you experience any of the following signs, it's probably time to reevaluate your short- and long-term career plans.

1. *Boredom.* Not having enough to do between assignments isn't so dangerous a sign as having no interest in the work you do have. You're ˎ

not likely to turn in your best job efforts if you don't care. It's better to realize that before your performance begins to deteriorate and your boss begins to notice. If you haven't suggested new projects that would interest you more to your boss or discussed other possibilities, do that now.

2. *Complaints.* If you're bending the ears of your family and friends with tales of woe or if you never talk about your job anymore, something is wrong. If you understand the reasons behind your complaints, you won't get too emotionally involved to do something about them.

3. *Not enough challenges.* If it's the same old routine every day, and you've stopped learning, it's time to develop new challenges. The question is whether you can do that within the confines of your job. Some jobs can be stretched to provide new opportunities as your skills develop; others are limited in their elasticity because of the structure of the department or organization. If your predecessors never did anything beyond the scope of the job description, it's likely that your boss doesn't encourage branching out and that a new position is the only way to get new learning opportunities.

4. *A deteriorating relationship with your boss.* Every relationship has its ups and downs, but, if yours has been on the skids for some time, it's important to figure out what went wrong. You may be able to make amends and get it back to where it once was if you make the effort. If the problem is the boss rather than you, you may simply have to wait out the situation.

5. *Lack of involvement.* Feeling that you're not part of the mainstream in your office can begin to have an impact on your work. You may feel left out because your department is often overlooked by management, or because you haven't asserted yourself, or because you simply don't fit in. It's important to discover which factor is behind your lack of involvement; if it's either of the first two, there are steps you can take to correct it; if it's the third, you may be better off getting out.

It's easy to slip into a lethargic, do-nothing attitude if you begin to resign yourself to unsatisfactory but tolerable work conditions. You'll know it's time to leave if your efforts to change the situation are ignored or rebuffed.

Your Second Job: What to Look For

Your first job has probably taught you as much about functioning in the working world as it has developed your skills. Your second job should offer you opportunities to build on your skills and acquire new ones. If you're interested in moving up, its important not to overstay Job One. You'll be much more attractive if you expand your experience to include areas with which you're not yet familiar.

People really on a fast track often make four or five moves before they reach 30. Each move is calculated to broaden their expertise and increase salary.

If you're offered a chance to try a job in a different area within your company, it's usually smart to accept that offer. Until you actually do it, it's easy to underestimate the quality of a job and even what you can learn from it. This kind of second job is often a lateral move — there's no salary increase or higher status involved. Lateral moves are much easier to make during the early years in your career, because your training is not that highly specialized.

Learning as much as you can about all aspects of a business puts you in a good position to move eventually into a management slot. In fact, formal management trainee courses deliberately expose trainees to all facets of a business, and participants are encouraged to spend a year or two in as many of them as they can. If your company doesn't have such a program or you're not in it, you can groom yourself for a better job by taking the same tack.

If your company posts job openings, check them regularly. If there's a particular department or job that appeals to you but you lack some of the prerequisites, ask the personnel department or the manager of the department how you can beef up your credentials. In some cases, the manager may be willing to train you. Don't be discouraged if you're not selected the first time you apply for a job in another area; find out what you can do to improve your chances the next time.

In smaller companies or those that don't post job openings, you'll have to let the personnel department or the manager know the areas in which you are interested in expanding your expertise.

Your second job should also be one that allows you to keep your options open. Even if you enjoyed your first job, don't overcommit yourself to that field. Ideally, your second job should prepare you for several related occupations. If, for example, your first job was assistant for a public relations firm, an ideal second job would combine copywriting (a technical skill), handling your own small accounts (an administrative skill), and periodically reviewing the work of the less experienced employees (a managerial skill). With skills translatable beyond the narrow area of public relations, you are more marketable and ultimately have more job choices — promotion/marketing department of a manufacturer, for example; community affairs division of a television station; or in-house publication unit of a large company.

If you did not enjoy your first job, the main thing you may have gotten from it was knowing what kind of job you don't want. It's important, however, to separate career dislikes from personal dislikes. If you didn't like your work but found other jobs within the company appealing, you're probably in the right field but in the wrong department or the wrong part of the business. You may be able to make a lateral move. Kate White moved from promotion copywriter on a magazine to an editorial writer by volunteering to write for the editorial section. When a job opened in that department, Kate applied for it and got it.

There are, of course, advantages to looking for your second job outside the company. One is that you'll probably be able to negotiate a higher salary. Corporate salary guidelines often prevent managers from raising an employee to a salary level commensurate with what he can receive in a similar job at another company. Another plus is seeing how another company works. You will be in a better position to judge the kind of management style that best suits you. Finally, since you will be working with a whole new group of people, you will be able to expand your contacts. The longer you work, the more important contacts become; they are the main source of information about job openings. You also may find you enjoy a higher status, even if the responsibilities are similar to the ones you could have had in your own company. Some people have a hard time shedding their "first-job" image of you.

If you decide to look for another job it pays to be discreet. Even trusted colleagues may unintentionally say something that can jeopardize your current position. When you're interviewing with prospective employers, tell them you would prefer they not check your references on your present position until they're ready to offer you the job. Most employers understand the need for confidentiality and will respect your request.

One of the major pitfalls of looking for a second job outside your company is that, even though it seems like a step up, it may in some respects not be as good as the job you left. Even if you asked questions about your specific responsibilities, it may be weeks or even months after you're on the job before you realize they aren't as challenging as you thought they would be. At that point, the only thing you can do is to make the best of it and initiate ways you might further expand your responsibilities.

Changing Fields: How Difficult Is It?

Career-hopping during their first few years is a common phenomenon among college graduates. Almost half change their career plans within five or six years after graduation. The most common reasons for considering a career switch are:

- Wanting to look for a job in your first-choice field after having had no success the first time around

- Having been unsure of what you wanted to do initially and having taken what sounded like an interesting job

- Becoming disillusioned about the field once you've had some experience

The American work force is a mobile one; even the second field you choose may not be the one you stay in for a lifetime. Here is a sample of the average tenures of people in various fields:

Civil engineers	13 years
Teachers	12 years
Physicians	11 years
Lawyers	10 years

Counselors . . . . 10 years
Management analysts . . 7 years
Securities salespersons . . 5 years

Before you decide to quit your job or start looking for a new one, determine what kind of job would suit you better. Then investigate job possibilities by talking to people who work in that field. You might call your alumni office for the names of recent graduates working in that field.

There's nothing wrong with taking a smorgasbord approach to your career, as long as each new job isn't an entry-level one. You will only end up frustrated, since you will never be in a field long enough to get a crack at the most exciting work. The ideal way is to build on each job experience — use at least some of the skills you developed in Job One to get into Job Two. The easiest way to do that is to switch to a closely related field.

After three years in television production, Erlene Berry Wilson switched to magazine editorial work. She promoted her skills that were common to both fields — initiating ideas, researching assignments, organizing material. A job change is not without trade-offs: Erlene had to take a cut in pay and status to get her foot in the door.

Changing job fields is always more difficult if neither your college experience nor your first job is at all related to the new field. Employers will understandably worry that your sudden interest may be short-lived. It may be especially hard to convince an employer if your academic work and first job experience is in a technical field — it may seem as if you're simply throwing it away, unless, of course, you can show how you plan to use it on the new job. If, for example, you're a dissatisfied engineer, you might consider a sales, supervisory, or administrative job rather than a straight technical job with an engineering firm.

Taking courses at a nearby college or university can give you a better idea of whether you would like a particular field. More and more adult educational divisions offer courses that feature working professionals who talk about their field and how to get into it. Courses that teach specific skills, such as computer programming, also can help you decide if you're really cut out for that kind of work. But don't commit yourself to a costly or time-consuming program until you check with personnel directors or department managers of companies for which you would like to work to find out if such a program or degree is a requirement.

Another way to test-market a field is to get involved before you look for a job. As a management trainee for an industrial service company, Michael Simon felt the only thing he was getting out of his job was a paycheck. He was interested in becoming a stockbroker but had no relevant academic background or job experience. He began on his own to study the annual reports and investor news. Nine months later, he successfully used his success with investing small amounts of his own money to sell his way into a broker position with a national firm.

The best way to determine your chances of switching into a different field is to interview with companies for which you'd like to work. The more specific your goal, the easier the transition. Don't rely on the interviewer's assessment of where your skills and experience might fit in; you might end up in a job that's wrong for you.

Getting Fired: It's Not the End of the World

Lily Tomlin was axed as a Howard Johnson's waitress when she glibly announced herself as "waitress of the week" over the restaurant's public-address system. When Richard Dreyfuss was part of a three-man comedy group, he was fired for insulting customers. Bestselling author Gail Sheehy lost a writing job when her editor found out she had been offered a better position at a competing newspaper.

Getting fired isn't the end of the world, nor will it necessarily block your chances of success. In fact, while it may be a temporary setback, it can mark a positive turn of events in your career.

Jack Snyder lost his first job as an elementary school teacher after two years because his academic credentials certified him to teach only high school. After the switch, he discovered he preferred teaching high school.

After one year, Bruce Browne was let go from his job in an accounting firm without being warned that his work was not up to par. In his second job in the accounting firm of a hospital, Bruce was given far more freedom and responsibility; after several months, his new employer told him they considered themselves lucky he had been fired from his first job.

The reason 25 percent of employees who leave — or are asked to leave — their first job do so is that they don't meet the standards of the job or don't fit into the company. That can be the employer's fault as much as the employee's. He may have misled you about the nitty-gritty responsibilities, or your expectations may have been out of line — a common first-job problem. In either case, if your lack of interest is evident in your attitude toward your work, your boss may look for an excuse to get rid of you.

If, in an effort to land a good job, you oversell your skills and can't catch on quickly enough, you also may be given your walking papers.

A third reason for getting canned is a personality conflict with the boss. Even though you seemed to click with each other during your job interviews, one of you misjudged the other's personality. It's difficult to know how you'll get along with someone until you start working with him. If the chemistry's bad, your employer probably will try to arrange a transfer for you. If not, the one comfort in getting fired for this reason is that it shouldn't hold you back from finding a new job quickly; the circumstances are understandable.

Ambitious people find themselves in the unemployment line, too. If your impatience gets the best of you and you get sloppy about the menial work you must do or project an I'm-too-good-for-this attitude, you may unconsciously be setting yourself up for dismissal. If you're a go-getter, you shouldn't have too much trouble landing another job, but, unless you learn how to control your ego, you may run into the same problem again.

Since no boss enjoys firing someone, he may decide to make your life so miserable you'll decide to leave. That's easier on your ego and your employment record and gives you time to look for another job, a luxury most firing bosses don't offer. On the other hand, a bad situation can drag on if you don't pick up on the signals, and unemployment compensation is usually unavailable if you "voluntarily" leave.

If you are fired, it's important to find out why, so you don't make the same mistake again. If your employer doesn't give you his reasons, ask — preferably at the time he tells you. If you're too upset, wait until you can collect yourself.

Even if you realize that getting fired was not your fault or that there was nothing you could have done to prevent it, your ego is likely to take a beating. Treat yourself to something you enjoy to get yourself in a better frame of mind. Bruce Browne spent a few weeks playing tennis.

If you can't afford to take a break, consider looking for temporary employment. Another alternative is filing for unemployment insurance. File right away, since it may be several weeks before you start collecting. Regulations governing unemployment vary from state to state; check with your local office to find out how long you must have worked, how much you must have earned, and whether you must have been officially let go. In some states you may collect if you quit because of intolerable working conditions (e.g., sexual harassment). You usually can collect unemployment for up to twenty-six weeks, but you must look actively for work, be available for full-time work, and agree to take a suitable job if one becomes available.

When you interview for your next job and are asked why you left your previous one, don't try to hide the circumstances; if the prospective employer is seriously considering you, he probably will want to contact your former employer. How much your former employer says depends on whether he knows your prospective employer and the circumstances under which you left. Generally, most employers confine their remarks to what you did well and omit what they view as your weaknesses. You needn't say, however, that you were fired; you can say that things didn't work out the way both of you had hoped or that it was a mutual parting of the ways. Denying you were fired can get you into trouble; if your employer finds out, even after you're hired, you may lose your credibility on your job.

Before you start interviewing for a new job, give some serious thought to what your next step ought to be. A lot will depend, of course, on how long you were in a first job. If you were there less than six months, you'll probably have to start out in another entry-level job. If, on the other hand, you have developed some specific skills, you may be left in a better position to market yourself than when you were looking for your first job.

Take your time looking for a new job. Don't take the first offer that comes along. If you're overanxious, the interviewer may think you're desperate to find a new job and begin to wonder why you aren't currently employed. If you act matter-of-factly about why you left your first job, the prospective employer is not likely to be too concerned about it.

Conclusion

Few first jobs measure up to expectations. Count yourself lucky if you are a little the wiser and can show an accomplishment or two. People are often reluctant to admit their jobs aren't working out as they'd hoped; they're reluctant to disappoint parents, former professors, or the person who got them the job; they're afraid of embarrassing themselves in front of friends who are doing much better. They view themselves as having failed a critical test of their abilities (and projecting, often erroneously, that this means they will fail in their second or third jobs as well).

Career strategies work fine on paper; in reality even the best-laid plans can go awry. It may be that you had an unrealistic notion of the field you entered, or that the company climate was distinctly out of sync with your personality, or that you found it impossible to deal with your boss.

The trick to coming out ahead, whether the unexpected is good or bad news, is to be flexible and to keep your options open. That means being willing to:

- Take the risk of changing fields or employers if the right opportunity comes your way.
- Accept a cut in pay if a new job offers more promise for the future than your current one.
- Walk away from a job that isn't advancing your career.
- Go into an area in which you have no formal training if it means an opportunity to learn new skills.

Being flexible also means developing patience. You may want to come on like gangbusters, but it's often better to sit tight and calculate your moves. Except for the few who get on a fast track because they're tops in a hot field or are in the right place at the right time, most young professionals don't take off in their careers for five to seven years. It takes time to develop expertise, build a reputation, get to know decision makers.

So, dig in and roll with the punches. Finding satisfaction and success in your career is no easy prospect: it takes time, hard work, and the ability to adapt. But true satisfaction in a career is worth working for, and it won't happen unless you lay the groundwork and stick around for the rewarding results.

Sources

Introduction:
Why Should You Read This Book?

America's Choice: High Skills or Low Wages! The Report of the Commission on the Skills of the American Workforce, National Center on Education and the Economy, June 1990.

Workforce 2000: Work and Workers for the 21st Century, by William B. Johnston and Arnold H. Packer et al., Hudson Institute, June 1987.

"A Greatly Improved Outlook for Graduates: A 1988 Update for the Year 2000," by Jon Sargent, *Occupational Outlook Quarterly,* U.S. Department of Labor, Bureau of Labor Statistics, Summer 1988.

"Surplus of College Graduates Dims Job Outlook for Others," by Louis Uchitelle, *New York Times,* June 18, 1990.

"The Chivas Regal Report on Working Americans: Emerging Values for the 1990s," conducted by Research & Forecasts, 1989.

Chapter 1: Careers

A Job in Your Major

"The Class of '84 One Year After Graduation," by Douglas J. Braddock and Daniel E. Hecker, *Occupational Outlook Quarterly,* Summer 1988.

Job Satisfaction After College . . . The Graduate's Viewpoint, by Ann Stouffer Bisconti and Lewis C. Solmon, College Placement Council Foundation, 1977.

Decision Making

"Thinking Clearly About Career Choices," by Irving Janis and Dan Wheeler, *Psychology Today,* May 1978.

Chapter 2: A Graduate Degree

Introduction

Employment Outcomes of Recent Master's and Bachelor's Degree Recipients, by the National Center for Educational Statistics, 1989.

A Second Degree

"Have MBA, Will Travel — Anywhere," by Monica Roman, *Business Week,* July 2, 1990.

"MBAs Trade Banking for Marketing," by Sandra Pesmen, *Advertising Age,* May 28, 1990.

"MBA May Not Be Worth It for Many Career-Switchers," by Amanda Bennett, *Wall Street Journal,* July 20, 1988.

When to Go to Grad School
Education in Industry, by Seymour Lusterman, Report No. 710, Conference Board, 1977.

Chapter 3: Employers

Whom to Work For
Your Rights at Work, by Darien McWhirter, John Wiley & Sons, 1989.

Fortune 500 or Small Business
Job Satisfaction After College . . . The Graduate's Viewpoint. (See earlier reference.)
Workforce 2000. (See earlier reference.)

On Your Own
Roper Campus Reports, June 1988.

Working Abroad
"How to Get a Job Overseas," by Peggy Schmidt, *New Woman,* June 1989.

Chapter 4: The Job Campaign

Resumes and Cover Letters
The 90-Minute Resume, by Peggy Schmidt, Peterson's Guides, 1990.
"Top a Strong Resume with a Great Cover Letter," by Peggy Schmidt, New York *Daily News,* June 6, 1988.

On-Campus Recruitment
"Campus Rites: The Job Interview," by Peggy Schmidt, *New York Times,* January 8, 1989.

Contacts
"Treat Contacts like Gold and They Will Pay Off," by Peggy Schmidt, New York *Daily News,* February 27, 1989.

Job Fairs
"Working the Floor at a Job Fair," by N. R. Kleinfield, *New York Times,* May 28, 1989.
"Fairs Offer Scores of Jobs Under One Convenient Roof," by Peggy Schmidt, New York *Daily News,* September 25, 1989.

Employment Agencies
"What to Do Before You Visit an Employment Agency," by Peggy Schmidt, New York *Daily News,* January 18, 1988.

Help-Wanted Ads
"Want Ads May Contain Some Pleasant Surprises," by Peggy Schmidt, New York *Daily News,* February 1, 1988.

Chapter 5: The Interview

Applications and Tests
Recruiting Trends 1989-90: A Study of Business, Industries, Governmental Agencies, and Educational Institutions Employing New College Graduates,

by L. Patrick Scheetz, Ph.D., Assistant Director, Career Development and Placement Services, Michigan State University.

The Northwestern Lindquist-Endicott Report 1990, by Victor R. Lindquist, The Placement Center, Northwestern University.

The Use of Integrity Tests for Pre-employment Screening, by the Office of Technology Assessment Project Staff (OTA-SET-442), U.S. Government Printing Office, September 1990.

"Lie-Detector Tests in a New Guise," by Peggy Schmidt, *New York Times,* October 1, 1989.

"Can You Pass the Job Test?" by Susan Dentzer et al., *Newsweek,* May 5, 1986.

"More Aid for Addicts on the Job," by Milt Freudenheim, *New York Times,* November 13, 1989.

Q and A: What You Will Be Grilled On and What to Ask
Employment Interviewing Quiz, Northeast Human Resources Association, 1988.

Rejection
The Northwestern Lindquist-Endicott Report 1990. (See earlier reference.)

Evaluating a Job Offer
Roper Campus Reports, June 1988.
America's Choice: High Skills or Low Wages. (See earlier reference.)

Chapter 7: Bosses

Boss Types
"Managing Your Boss," by John J. Gabarro and John P. Kotter, *Harvard Business Review,* January-February 1980.

The Most Common Boss Problems
"Managers Can Drive Their Subordinates Mad," by Manfred F. R. Kets de Vries, *Harvard Business Review,* July-August 1979.

"The Subordinate's Predicaments," by Eric H. Neilsen and Jan Gypen, *Harvard Business Review,* September-October 1979.

"The Abrasive Personality at the Office," by Harry Levinson, *Psychology Today,* May 1978.

Women Bosses: Advice for Men
"Women in Corporate Management," *Catalyst,* June 1990.

Mentors
Breaking the Glass Ceiling, by Ann M. Morrison, Randall P. White, Ellen Van Velsor, and the Center for Creative Leadership, Addison Wesley, 1987.

Chapter 8: Office Politics

Brownnosing
"Kiss, Kiss, Grovel, Grovel — How Far Should a Man Go to Flatter His Boss?" by Harry Stein, *Esquire,* October 1979.

Enemies
Jane Trahey on Women and Power, by Jane Trahey, Rawson Associates
  Publishers, 1977.

Chapter 10: Ethics

Introduction
"What Bosses Think About Corporate Ethics," by Timothy D.
  Schellhardt, *Wall Street Journal,* April 6, 1988.

Petty Theft on the Job
Thieves at Work: An Employer's Guide to Combating Workplace Dishonesty,
  by I. Shepard and R. Duston, U.S. Bureau of National Affairs, 1988.
*Dishonesty in the Workplace: A Manager's Guide to Preventing Employee
  Theft,* by Richard C. Hollinger and John P. Clark, London House Press,
  1989.
"Summary Overview of the 'State of the Art' Regarding Information
  Gathering Techniques and Level of Knowledge in Three Areas Con-
  cerning Crime Against Business," American Management Associa-
  tion, March 1977.

Lying
Lying: Moral Choice in Public and Private Life, by Sissela Bok, Vintage
  Books, 1978.
"Conflicts: Concealing the Truth for a Good Reason," by Ruth Macklin
  and Tabitha M. Powledge, *Savvy,* January 1980.
"What Business Thinks About Employee Rights," by David W. Ewing,
  Harvard Business Review, September-October 1977.

Whistle-Blowing
"Whistle Blower's Anguish," by Don Oldenburg, *Washington Post,*
  March 31, 1987.
Individual Rights in the Corporation: A Reader of Employee Rights, ed. by
  Alan F. Westin and Stephan Salisbury, Random House, 1980.

Chapter 11: Discrimination

Introduction
"Women and Minorities: Is Industry Ready?" by Peggy Schmidt, *New
  York Times,* October 16, 1988.
"A Slap at Sex Stereotypes," *Time,* May 15, 1989.

Job Inequities
*Know Your Rights: What You Should Know About Equal Employment Oppor-
  tunity,* Equal Employment Opportunity Commission, September
  1976.

Taming Office Wolves
"Outcomes of Sexual Harassment Charges," by David E. Terpstra and
  Douglas D. Baker, *Academy of Management Journal,* March 1988.

Filing a Suit
Your Rights at Work, by Darien McWhirter, John Wiley & Sons, 1989.

Chapter 12: Moving On

Introduction
Job Satisfaction After College . . . The Graduate's Viewpoint. (See earlier reference.)

Promotion
College and Other Stepping Stones: A Study of Learning Experiences That Contribute to Effective Performance in Early and Long-Run Jobs, by Ann Stouffer Bisconti, The College Placement Council Foundation, 1980.

Job Dissatisfaction
Job Satisfaction After College . . . The Graduate's Viewpoint. (See earlier reference.)

Your Second Job
"Industry Hoppers Move Ahead," by Peggy Schmidt, *New York Times,* April 16, 1989.

Changing Fields
College and Other Stepping Stones. (See earlier reference.)

Getting Fired
Current Biography, January 1976.
"Getting Fired Can Be the Start of Something Big," by Peggy Schmidt, New York *Daily News,* March 7, 1988.

Conclusion

College and Other Stepping Stones. (See earlier reference.)
Job Satisfaction After College . . . The Graduate's Viewpoint. (See earlier reference.)

About the Author

Peggy Schmidt, author of the bestselling book *The 90-Minute Resume*, writes a syndicated newspaper column, "Your New Job," and has been a career columnist for *Glamour* and *New Woman* magazines. As career coordinator for the New York University Summer Publishing Institute, Schmidt has counseled hundreds of recent college graduates on how to find their first job.